Mastering
DOCUMENT
ANALYSIS

A 3-Step Approach to Finding the Past

by Tony Maccarella

SHERPALEARNING
GUIDING YOU TO EVEN GREATER HEIGHTS

Sherpa Learning is dedicated to helping high-achieving learners gain access to high-quality, skills-based instruction that is created, reviewed, and tested by teachers. To learn more about Sherpa Learning and our vision, or to learn about some of our upcoming projects, please visit us at www.sherpalearning.com.

Publisher/Editor: David Nazarian

Copy-Editor: Christine DeFranco

Cartographer: Sal Esposito

Cover Design: Nazarian/Maccarella

Cover Image: photo by badahos, ©shutterstock.com

ISBN 978-0-9905471-7-4

Copyright © 2019
Sherpa Learning, LLC.
West Milford, New Jersey
www.sherpalearning.com

Printed in the United States of America.

10 9 8 7 6 5 4 3 2 1

For Mia
Live the life you dream!

Table of Contents

Table of Contents

Finding the Past

When I first started teaching, two events permanently changed the way I do my job.

I was hanging out with my college friends one summer afternoon comparing how far we'd come in the first couple of years since graduation. It was 1985, and one guy was working for GE Aerospace making more than $50K (not bad for a 25 year old in 1985), another was a bank auditor making about $35,000, and I was a high school teacher in my third year making $14,100. Of the three of us, I was the only one who had attended college on an academic scholarship and graduated with a GPA better than 3.0. My old roommate, Choo-Choo, commenting on the apparent inequity of our salaries, made the point that although I made significantly less than my buddies, I at least had the easiest job of everyone there. I only worked half-days, had summers off, and because I taught history, I "only had to learn the story one time because it never changes"—so the rest of my career was going to be a cakewalk!

Although Choo's comment was in good fun and we all had a great laugh, there was something about it that really bothered me, not just as a teacher, but as a history professional. I didn't mind that he had inadvertently underestimated the value of teaching or the impact that my career choice might have on thousands of young people. I was, even then, already accustomed to this misperception of the profession. But the notion of history as some story that "never changes" just seemed like much more than an understatement. It was a complete misunderstanding of my chosen field of study and I knew it would forever change the way I approached teaching history. From that moment forward, I vowed to reevaluate my instructional practices, seeking ways to help my students learn what History really is—a never-ending struggle to make sense of the past. I was largely unsuccessful, until a second career-changing event occurred.

I lived with my grandparents in those early years of my career. It was mostly for the sake of convenience—mine *and* theirs. I happily accepted my grandmother's delicious meals and free laundry service, and they enjoyed having a live-in handyman and someone who could reach the top shelf in the kitchen cabinet. One day my grandfather presented me with a special gift from the infinite pieces of memorabilia he had saved over his lifetime of nearly 80 years. It was a flag.

He opened a little box and pulled out a Japanese flag from the Second World War. The story he told me about that then-40-year-old artifact was brief but intriguing, and it became the centerpiece of the WWII unit in my U.S. History course. According to my grandfather, who had not personally served in the war, the flag was given to him by a good friend who had fought in the Pacific Theater. His friend said that he had taken the flag, "off the body of a dead Japanese soldier." My grandfather even showed me a stain that appeared to be a bloodstain, no doubt from the dead enemy. In addition to the stain, the flag was covered in Japanese characters— presumably words of valor and patriotism to encourage the flag bearer to "Fight to the Death" and "Never Surrender!"

All of this information fit neatly into the story of the Pacific Theater of WWII as it was portrayed in my U.S. History textbook, and as I understood it to be true from *both* years of

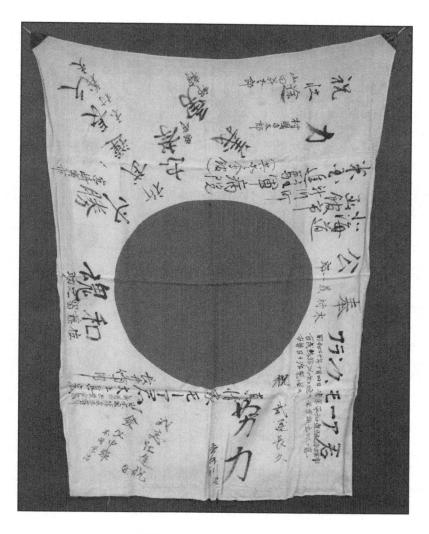

undergraduate U.S. History courses. Year after year, I would show the flag to my students and convey my grandfather's story, and we would begin to discuss the mentality of the Japanese military and the "never-surrender" attitude that inspired our leaders to use weapons of mass destruction in an attempt to save millions of U.S. soldiers in a conflict that might otherwise have dragged on for months.

Then one day… *history happened.* It was 1989 and one of my 121 students was a Japanese exchange student. An exuberant junior who enjoyed everything American, she did all she could to be a major part of every class discussion. I approached her early in the year, months before our WWII unit, and asked if she might be able to translate the characters on my flag. I was certain it could only enhance the story of WWII and the Pacific front. Having not yet heard my flag story, my exchange student could not have known the impact of her work as she came smiling into class the next morning and handed me the flag and a folded piece of paper with all the translations.

Here is what was written on the paper:

Dear Frank More,

October 4, 1946

American military came and showed us their faith to Hakodate City

People welcomed them and the whole city was full of life

(signed) Giichiro Kimura

Beikoku Shinchu Gun (American Hospital)

Kyowakaikan

Togawacho, Hakodate City, Hokkaido

Power! (signed) Kichitaro Murakuni

Celebration! Courage! Loyalty!

Mind. Officially. Blown!

A flood of questions washed over me in the minutes after I read that folded paper. How could this be? Why did my grandfather tell me that story? Had he invented it or was it created by his friend, Frank? Why would anyone have lied about the origin of this flag? How does this new information fit into my understanding of the Pacific Theater? What else has been misunderstood?

Despite my firm belief that Choo-Choo was completely misguided in his assessment of my profession back in 1985, I somehow had continued my first few years of teaching according to the very assumption I knew to be incorrect! I was still teaching history as if it were a story that only had to be learned once. That day, the foundation of my professional approach to teaching history was shaken to its core by one of my students. I realized that I had to start doing things differently—very differently.

For the first time, when my class studied the Second World War, I used my flag, and the story of discovering its true meaning, to illustrate that history was not just some story that you learn. **History is really a struggle to find the past through an analysis of the limited evidence left behind by those who came before us.** Even at 16 years old, my students had something to contribute to this search. My flag no longer served as a mere museum exhibit; it was now a springboard into several conversations about our understanding of WWII. Why were the Japanese soldiers who wrote on this flag so enamored with my grandfather's friend, Frank? Was their attitude representative of the majority in Japan less than one year removed from Hiroshima and Nagasaki? If so, what does that add to our discussion of the ethics of using weapons of mass destruction? Why did Frank feel it was necessary to lie to my grandfather about the origins of his flag? What was the historical context within the United States that might have contributed to Frank's reluctance to share his story of friendship with Japanese comrades in arms—even with one of his best friends? These are the kinds of questions that have kept me in this profession for over 35 years, and these are the kinds of questions that, at least since 1989, I have tried to inspire my students to ask of the evidence before them.

History class should not be a passive *story* about the past—the excitement in History is in *finding* the past.

Why Documents Matter

Students of history must analyze all sorts of evidence—my Japanese flag is only one small example. More often than not, historical evidence takes the form of written documents, photographs, and artwork. Documents like these are at the heart of the study of history. They make my job exciting and ever-changing because historians are constantly discovering new documents and reevaluating old ones. With each new discovery or interpretation, "the story" of history is challenged. This process never ends because we can never know every circumstance surrounding key moments in history. As new documents shed new light on old stories, we begin to understand past moments from a different perspective, encouraging fresh debate.

A great example of the impact documents have on our understanding of history involves the story of Michelangelo and the Sistine Chapel. Already, you have probably conjured scenes in your mind of the Renaissance painter, probably in a puffy hat, lying on his back with a brush extended up to the ceiling just inches away from his face. The "Michelangelo painting on his back" story has become common lore in World History classes across the country. In fact, many of my past students probably have fond memories of lying on their backs on the classroom floor, painting on paper taped to the underside of their desks. It was a fun way to gain some insight into the process followed by one of the world's greatest artists. Unfortunately, the entire lesson was probably based on an inaccurate story. In his engaging book, *Michelangelo and the Pope's Ceiling*, Ross King traces the mistake back to a document written all the way back in 1527. About that time, Paolo Giovio, the bishop of Nocera, wrote a brief biography of Michelangelo entitled *Michaelis Angeli Vita* (The Life of Michelangelo). In this work, Giovio described the painter's posture on the scaffold as *resupinus*, which means "bent backward." The description has been frequently mistranslated as "on his back," and this error is likely responsible for the image most people have of Michelangelo painting the ceiling of the Sistine Chapel. According to King, the physical evidence inside the chapel, as well as Michelangelo's own sketches of his scaffolding, make it more likely that the painter stood atop his platform with his arms above his head and "bent backward" to see the evolving fresco on the ceiling.

Documents are the key to understanding history, but even so, they create as many questions as answers. Where did the document originate? What was its original purpose? For whom was it originally intended? What else was happening in that place at that time? How might the original audience have interpreted it? How did we come to know of this document? In what ways does the document add to or alter the "story" as we understand it thus far? To answer these questions and make the best use of the documentary evidence available to us in the field of history, we must have a systematic way of analyzing those documents. That is the purpose of this book.

What is Document Analysis

If historians were archaeologists, documents would be the artifacts they find at a dig site. If historians were scientists, documents would be their experimental data. Documents form the foundation of our study of history and document analysis is the way we build our stories upon that foundation. Therefore, document analysis is the most important thing in the historian's toolbox.

Even if you never intend to become a professional historian, the skills necessary to do document analysis are essential to becoming **a more discerning reader**. Whether you are reading historical documents or the current news of the world, whether you are in middle school or a college senior, whether you are writing a thesis essay or arguing about politics at the dinner table, you will be more successful if you invest time in developing and honing good document analysis skills.

Moving Forward

So now you understand how historians use evidence to find the past and why documents comprise the biggest piece of that historical evidence. You've seen that document analysis is the most important task in the historian's job description, and that the skills of document analysis are essential to the study of history. In Unit 1, you will be introduced to a 3-step process for developing your own document analysis skills. Fear not! Each step is explained in detail and samples are provided all along the way.

The 3-Step Process

Document analysis can seem like a daunting task, but you can master this skill by following a simple 3-step process—Summarize, Analyze, Criticize. When you **summarize** a document, you briefly explain *WHAT* the document says—you paraphrase. To **analyze**, you must tell *HOW* or *WHY* the document is important. Analysis is easiest when the document must support a specific thesis, but as long as you have defined "important," you'll be able to analyze the document. **Criticize** is short for "critically analyzing the source of the document,"—essentially, identifying its point-of-view. This last step is the most often overlooked part of the process, but it is essential if you want to improve the sophistication of your arguments, something that holds great value in college and in life.

If these steps are applied in the prewriting segment of an essay, you will find you have everything necessary to support your thesis. Simply put, good document analysis skills will help you to write better essays. Practicing those skills will improve the speed, ease, and quality of those essays. It's a simple formula that works and will result in much less agony when facing a document based essay.

Summarize

A summary can be described as the main idea of the document. This idea is rarely stated explicitly within the text of the document itself, but rather implied by the text as a whole. Consequently, summarizing is definitely not a copy-and-paste skill, but, with practice, it is a skill that can be mastered by anyone.

Analyze

Analysis is a strange concept for many students. When I ask students to tell me what it means to analyze, few can actually put a definition into words. Even students who are excellent at analyzing struggle to actually define the term. Analysis can be defined as a statement that answers the question, "Why does this document matter (to history or to my thesis)?" If you are writing an essay based on documents (DBQ), analytical statements will tell how or why each document supports the thesis. If you are practicing document analysis in isolation, (without an essay question), you need to formulate a definition of "importance"—why should the document matter? The answer to that question is your analysis of the document.

Criticize

The final step, criticize, is essential to any sophisticated argument supported by outside evidence. A critical analysis of the document's source demonstrates an understanding that all written evidence is influenced by the author, audience, purpose, and historical context. Even university students often have a very difficult time with critical analysis, so don't be surprised if you find the concept confusing at first. Confusing or not, however, critical analysis is essential to a complete understanding of the document, and, like the other two steps, it is a skill that can be mastered with practice.

Part 1: Summarize

When my daughter, Mia, turned thirteen, she went with about ten of her friends to see the movie *Divergent*. When she came home that night, I asked, "So tell me what the movie was about?" For the next 90 minutes, I listened to a blow-by-blow recounting of *Divergent*, complete with character dialogue and eighth-grader film review notes. Summarizing is difficult.

I've heard many teachers (usually the old, crotchety ones) explain the difficulty as a result of the laziness of "kids these days." It's been a long time since I was Mia's age, but I definitely had better summary skills, as did my peers and classmates. So was I really less lazy? I don't think so, and I'm pretty sure my mom would agree. My friends and I disliked spending a lot of time doing homework just as much as you. So what can explain the differences between summary skills in the old days and those of "kids these days?" Were my teachers better? Probably not. Were we all just smarter back then? Unlikely.

Maybe the difference is in the historical context. When I was a kid, there was no internet. There weren't even any computers yet! If I had to do research for a school report or an essay, I was forced to spend time physically inside of a library. I can assure you that today's libraries are like amusement parks compared with libraries back in the day, so I wanted to get out of there as quickly as possible. I would start at the card catalog (the big cabinet with tiny drawers usually used as a display table today) and then follow the Dewey Decimal numbers to some huge reference book that included a few pages about my topic and was restricted to onsite use. I only needed the main ideas from this book, but there was no way for me to "capture" that information quickly—no photocopy machines or digital cameras. My choice was either to hand-copy pages of text, word-for-word (think: medieval monk), or to find a way to discern the essence of that text and write only that brief idea. Those of us in that earlier generation became excellent paraphrasers, not because of our dedication

3

to developing better research skills, but rather because of our laziness (hereafter referred to as "efficiency"). It took less time to write one or two sentences than it did to copy dozens of lengthy paragraphs. It is precisely this desire for "efficiency" that has led today's generation of teenagers to lose the ability to summarize a text quickly and easily—who needs to write a summary when you can just scan a page with your phone? Following are several techniques designed to help you remedy this shortcoming.

The Cover-up

This is a great technique for training your brain to stop "lifting" details when you summarize. If you were asked right now to read the paragraph above and summarize its main point, it is likely that your "summary" would include words and phrases like *paraphrasing*, *photocopiers*, *laziness*, and *word-for-word*. None of these terms are necessary to a good summary of the paragraph, and, in fact, any summary that attempted to include these words in context would need to be several sentences and would still likely miss the point of the paragraph. The main point of the previous paragraph was that it was easier for past generations of students to learn to summarize. Unfortunately, when today's students are asked to summarize a paragraph that they just read, their first instinct is to look back and reread. Rereading the paragraph assumes that you misunderstood it the first time, and rereading is most likely to lead you to spot important-looking terms and copy them onto your paper.

The Cover-up technique simply requires that you read a paragraph only once, cover it completely (with your hand or a piece of paper), and write a short phrase that you believe captures the essence of what you just read. It's not easy, and you may find it nearly impossible at first—as though your mind has gone blank. After some practice, however, you will find that summarizing is quite natural, and likely as "efficient" as copying and pasting.

Example 1.1:

Directions: Read the document, then cover it with your hand and write a one-line summary of the main idea.

Document A

Le Hao, the prefect (governor) of Dunhuang [a Silk Road town at the eastern edge of the Taklamakan Desert], had supplied them with the means of crossing the desert, in which there are many evil demons and hot winds. Travelers who encounter them perish all to a man. There is not a bird to be seen in the air above, nor an animal on the ground below. Though you look all round most earnestly to find where you can cross, you know not where to make your choice, the only mark and indication being the dry bones of the dead left upon the sand.

SOURCE: Faxian, Chinese Buddhist monk, from his account of his travels along the Silk Road, c. 400 CE

If you wrote something like, "There are evil demons and hot winds in the desert" it would seem like "demons" and "winds" are the subject of the document. You might have said, "Lots of people die in the desert," and that is clearly stated in the document, but that's only one smaller point. We're looking for the main point. What is the author really saying?

Although this brief document contains several fascinating details about travel on the Silk Road, including an allusion to supernatural beings, the point of this passage can be stated in a single sentence: *The Taklamakan Desert was difficult to cross.* How closely did your summary match this one?

The Up-goer Five Text Editor

A truly unique tool for improving paraphrasing skills is called The Up-goer Five Text Editor. A webcomic artist named Randall Munroe attempted to "translate" technical diagrams of the Saturn V rocket into "commonly used words in everyday life." He included only the one thousand most frequently used words. Intrigued by this, Theo Sanderson at Splasho.com created a text editor that forces users to restrict their vocabulary to the top "ten hundred" words (*thousand* isn't one of them). This can be a great tool to use for the purpose of summarizing, because it completely eliminates the possibility of just lifting details in a cut-and-paste format. By using The Up-goer Five Text Editor, you are prevented from copying most details—even if you wanted to—because every word must be included within the most-frequently used one thousand words. This technique will often result in a phrase that is a somewhat less accurate representation of the main idea than that which you can create using the Cover-Up, but working through the Up-goer Five process is certain to give you a better understanding of the document.

Example 1.2:

Directions: Read the document, and then use The Up-goer Five Text Editor to write a one-line summary of the main idea. You can find the text editor at http://splasho.com/upgoer5.

Document B

Every morning a girl comes and brings a tub of water, and places it before her master. In this he proceeds to wash his face and hands, and then his hair, combing it out over the vessel. Thereupon he blows his nose, and spits into the tub, and, leaving no dirt behind, conveys it all into this water. When he has finished, the girl carries the tub to the man next to him, who does the same. Thus she continues carrying the tub from one to another till each of those who are in the house has blown his nose and spit into the tub, and washed his face and hair.

SOURCE: Ibn Fadlan, a Muslim envoy to the Kingdom of the Bulgars in Eastern Europe, from his account of the Viking Rus living along the Volga River within present-day Russia, 922 CE

Again, the document is filled with details that may have distracted you from the main point— the Viking Rus all wash in the same tub. Of course, your Up-goer Five summary may have looked more like this: *These men all cleaned in the same water.* Was your summary similar to this one?

Visualize It

Another way to overcome the difficulty of rewording the main idea of a document is to "unword" the summary. Read the document first, and then draw images to represent the main points. If the document is long and contains a series of points, you might create a cartoon strip in which each frame represents a paragraph within the document. For shorter documents, however, a single drawing will be fine.

The best way to do this activity is with a partner or a small group. Each of you start with a different document that no one else can see. Draw your main idea image, and then exchange your drawings. See if your partner can figure out the main idea of your document from the sketch alone. If you include too many details in your drawing, your partner might miss the main idea entirely. It might be tricky at first, but this is a great way to practice the art of summarization, and it's almost always laugh-out-loud fun—like Pictionary for history geeks.

Example 1.3:

Directions: Read the document, and then sketch an image that summarizes the main idea.

Document C

Moreover they need no commissariat, nor the conveyance of supplies, for they have with them sheep, cows, horses, and the like quadrupeds, the flesh of which they eat, naught else. As for their beasts which they ride, these dig into the earth with their hoofs and eat the roots of plants, knowing naught of barley. And so, when they alight anywhere, they have need of nothing from without. As for their religion, they worship the sun when it rises, and regard nothing as unlawful, for they eat all beasts, even dogs, pigs, and the like.

SOURCE: Ibn al-Athir, a Muslim historian, from his eyewitness account of the Mongol invasion of western Asia, c. 1231 CE

No one drawing is exactly correct, but any image that implies the self-sufficiency of the Mongols would be accurate.

Part 2: Analyze

Analysis is certainly more difficult than summary, but the inherent difficulty is further complicated by the fact that students often confuse the concept of analysis with that of interpretation (which is more closely akin to summary). The distinction between Summarize and Analyze, in the context of this book, is that one answers the question, "What does the document say?" (Summarize), and the second answers the question, "Why does the document matter?" (Analyze). In this context, *interpretation* (What does the document mean?) is much more like a summary. **Analysis involves connecting the document with other ideas to demonstrate its importance.** Connections may be made with other events in history, key concepts of an era, causal or correlational hypotheses, or other documents; but in every case, the connection is the key to good analysis.

Sometimes your teachers add to the confusion — often, ironically, in an attempt to clarify. Maybe you've been asked to use acronyms in class to help you remember the many pieces of what we call "analysis". The problem is that most of these acronyms are actually mashups of summary, analysis, and critical analysis— all together.* Acronyms, like SOAPS, SOAPSTone, PERSIA, and others, can be excellent tools for a discussion of the various facets of a document. I've used some of these detailed tools myself, but too often my students have failed to connect the dots. Even after they've answered the specific questions associated with each acronym, they were unable to use those answers to assemble a thorough understanding of the document and its importance in the context of history. Having experienced this disconnect firsthand for many years, I began to reformulate the questions I asked in class so that I might simplify the process and transcend the morass. This was the birth of the *MDA* approach — Summarize, Analyze, Criticize.

For my colleagues who may be reading this and preparing to toss it down with a firm "Rubbish!" please suspend your disbelief for just a moment longer.

Analysis, then, is quite simply based on a single question — "Why does this matter?" Use all the acronyms you want, but eventually those details must lead back to that one question. Any discussion of why a document matters is likely to lead to some lively in-class debate about *why it should matter*. These discussions of historical significance are at the core of good history. When you attempt to make sense of a document within the context of what you already know about an historical period, or use a document to raise questions for further research, you are thinking like a professional historian. Learning historical thinking skills is a priority in every history class.

In order to answer the question, "Why does it matter?" you must ask yourself two other questions. "What do I know about the time period within which this document was created?" and "In what ways does my summary of this document support or challenge my understanding of this time period?" Depending on your purpose for analyzing the document in the first place these questions may change slightly. The basic point of the activity, however, will always be to connect the summary of the document with your understanding of its historical context. In doing so, try to focus primarily on the content of the document itself, rather than the source. An analysis of the source is the focus of our third step, Criticize.

Example 2.1:

Directions: Read Document A again and think about your summary. If you were answering an essay question that required you to "assess the difficulties associated with trading along the Silk Road," why might this document be important to your answer?

Document A

Le Hao, the prefect (governor) of Dunhuang [a Silk Road town at the eastern edge of the Taklamakan Desert], had supplied them with the means of crossing the desert, in which there are many evil demons and hot winds. Travelers who encounter them perish all to a man. There is not a bird to be seen in the air above, nor an animal on the ground below. Though you look all round most earnestly to find where you can cross, you know not where to make your choice, the only mark and indication being the dry bones of the dead left upon the sand.

SOURCE: Faxian, Chinese Buddhist monk, from his account of his travels along the Silk Road, c. 400 CE

Remember that our summary of Document A was that The Taklamakan Desert was difficult to cross. An assessment of the impediments to trade along the Silk Road would certainly be enhanced by direct support from a contemporary Silk Road traveler. Additionally, a second look at the document would reveal several details supporting that contention: people said evil demons lived there, there are few birds or animals that can live there, the bones of unsuccessful travelers can be seen, and no obvious route across this desert is apparent. Using our general statement of summary and these details, we are able to connect this document with our response to the essay question—that is why it matters!

Example 2.2:

Directions: Read Document B again and think about your summary. What do you know about the Vikings already? Make a general statement about the character of a Viking community based on your previous studies. Does Document B tend to support your statement, or does it contradict? In what ways does it corroborate or contradict your characterization of the Vikings?

Document B

Every morning a girl comes and brings a tub of water, and places it before her master. In this he proceeds to wash his face and hands, and then his hair, combing it out over the vessel. Thereupon he blows his nose, and spits into the tub, and, leaving no dirt behind, conveys it all into this water. When he has finished, the girl carries the tub to the man next to him, who does the same. Thus she continues carrying the tub from one to another till each of those who are in the house has blown his nose and spit into the tub, and washed his face and hair.

SOURCE: Ibn Fadlan, a Muslim envoy to the Kingdom of the Bulgars in eastern Europe, from his account of the Viking Rus living along the Volga River within present-day Russia, 922 CE

Earlier, we summarized this document as "Viking men washed in the same tub." When you studied the Vikings in class, you may have concluded that, as a group, Viking warriors are a tough bunch. Although this document does not directly address their "toughness," it seems that Ibn Fadlan views them as rather rough and even uncouth, both qualities that might support your characterization that they were "a tough bunch."

Example 2.3:

Directions: Read Document C again and consider the summary implied by your drawing in the exercise above. If you were researching for a paper or project about Mongol warfare, do you think that this document could be considered important within the context of your research?

Document C

Moreover they need no commissariat, nor the conveyance of supplies, for they have with them sheep, cows, horses, and the like quadrupeds, the flesh of which they eat, naught else. As for their beasts which they ride, these dig into the earth with their hoofs and eat the roots of plants, knowing naught of barley. And so, when they alight anywhere, they have need of nothing from without. As for their religion, they worship the sun when it rises, and regard nothing as unlawful, for they eat all beasts, even dogs, pigs, and the like.

SOURCE: Ibn al-Athir, a Muslim historian, from his eyewitness account of the Mongol invasion of western Asia, c. 1231 CE

Remember that we drew pictures illustrating the self-sufficiency of the Mongol armies. Any paper or project about Mongol warfare would need to explain how they conquered so many people and so much territory in so little time. Since armies must always contend with the logistics of supplying food and fuel to the soldiers, do you think that a document detailing the ways by which the Mongol warriors were able to maintain their food and fuel supplies on-the-go might be important to an analysis of the success and speed of their armies?

Part 3: Criticize

Critical analysis— it even sounds difficult. Because most students do not really understand the concept, they make it more difficult than it has to be. The first point to make clear is that critical analysis is an analysis of the SOURCE of the document, not the document itself. Some students think their task is to answer the question, "What does it really say?" Others think that critical analysis implies "evaluation" or answering, "How do I feel about what the document says?" In fact, critical analysis is a process by which we recognize that all documents are the products of people, and those people are all influenced by the world around them, their intentions, and their personal experiences. These "biases" are inevitable and uncontrollable; there is no "unbiased" or "objective" document.

When you "criticize" the document, you analyze the source and connect it to the words in the document and the context of the world from which it came. For this task, you must consider the following questions:

- Who is the author?
- What do I know about him/her?
- What do I know about his/her time period?
- What do I know about his/her geographical setting?
- Why was this document written/published?
- Why might this author have written these words in this way?

The answers to these questions help historians—and history students—to better understand the significance and impact of the document. Historians call it contextualization, but we call it Criticize.

The Criticize task is somewhat speculative. Can we really know why an author might have said or written the words in a document? Motives, intent, and even the impact of personal experience are almost impossible to know with any certainty. We can, however, speculate answers to these questions based on evidence we know about the author and the historical setting. Instead of attempting to identify a definite "bias" in a document, it is more important to suggest ways by which the source may have been influenced to create this particular document. Your suggestion need not be absolutely true to be useful, but it must be reasonable and relevant. For example, it is reasonable to suggest that a document written by Martin Luther in 1518 may have been influenced by his religious beliefs or his experiences with the Roman Catholic Church. If you can connect that suggestion with the content of the document, then it may also be relevant.

Be careful to avoid "preachy" personal assessments of the document or its author in this step. Students often spend time assessing the validity of a document based on the author's "bias." As stated at the outset, all authors are biased and, therefore, all documents are the products of bias. There are no objective, unbiased documents, so get over it! This is not to say that the question of reliability is unhelpful. On the contrary, suggestions about the reliability of documents can, and should, be an essential part of historical analysis. It is, instead, the vilification of the word, bias, that is the problem.

Example 3.1:

Directions: Consider our summary of Document C, "The Mongol armies were self-sufficient." Reread the document and think about that point, as well as the tone of the language used.

Document C

Moreover they need no commissariat, nor the conveyance of supplies, for they have with them sheep, cows, horses, and the like quadrupeds, the flesh of which they eat, naught else. As for their beasts which they ride, these dig into the earth with their hoofs and eat the roots of plants, knowing naught of barley. And so, when they alight anywhere, they have need of nothing from without. As for their religion, they worship the sun when it rises, and regard nothing as unlawful, for they eat all beasts, even dogs, pigs, and the like.

SOURCE: Ibn al-Athir, a Muslim historian, from his eyewitness account of the Mongol invasion of western Asia, c. 1231 CE

Now, look at the source and answer the following questions:

1. What do you know about the author, Ibn al-Athir?

2. What do you know about Muslims of the early 13th century?

3. What do you know about the Mongols of the early 13th century?

4. What do you know about the Mongol invasion of western Asia?

5. Why might Ibn al-Athir have conveyed this tone in his writing about the Mongols?

6. Why might Ibn al-Athir have devoted time to a description of the self-sufficiency of the Mongols?

It is unlikely that you know much about Ibn al-Athir himself. Even history teachers who use his writings as evidence in class rarely spend too much time discussing the details of his life. He is described as a Muslim historian, however, and you may know something about Muslims and historians. You may remember that Muslims, even in what Europeans call the Middle Ages, were very particular about their food and their religion. In fact, Islam was the governing force in the lives of thirteenth-century Muslims. On the other hand, you may have learned in your study of Genghis Khan that he and the other Mongols were very un-particular about religious concerns. In fact, Mongol rulers generally accepted all religions. You may also remember that Mongols were nomadic herders and originated in the harsh Asian steppe land, where agriculture was difficult, if not impossible.

Regarding Mongol invasions, you may have heard of their attack on the Khwarezmian (Persian) empire. This battle is the origin of Genghis Khan's famous quote, "I am the scourge of God." Did you know that the Khwarezmian people were Muslims? Did you know that the siege of the Khwarezmian capital took place in 1220— 11 years prior to Ibn al-Athir's account of it? Did you know that Ibn al-Athir probably witnessed the attack firsthand, or at least heard details of it shortly after it happened? Do you think that Ibn al-Athir's personal experiences with the Mongol armies might have influenced his writing? Why might he have employed a tone of disgust when describing the self-sufficiency of the Mongols in Document C?

In light of his tone, why do you think Ibn al-Athir even bothered to say that the Mongol army was so self-sufficient?

It may be that Ibn al-Athir was so shocked by the defeat of the Khwarezmian Empire by this band of barbarians that he needed to find some way to mitigate the outcome. By describing the Mongols as completely without need of a supply chain, Ibn al-Athir was able to justify their unusual speed and efficiency. Additionally, if he could convey that the Mongols were "uncivilized," he might be better able to explain the brutality of their attack. The Mongols were brutal barbarians without morals or even a soul, and so the great Khwarezmian Muslim soldiers, governed by the laws of God and the rules of war, were incapable of defending themselves.

Moving Forward

At this point, you may feel like you're ready for a spot in the Princeton University History Department, but although the *MDA* 3-Step Process is simple to understand, you will need practice applying that process to the analysis of various kinds of historical documents. Each of the remaining units is devoted to the analysis of a unique type of document. Units 2 and 3 apply the 3-Step Process to firsthand accounts, like letters and newspaper articles. Units 4 and 5 deal with the special challenges associated with the analysis of literary and visual documents. Finally, Unit 6 helps you to apply the *MDA* process to secondary source documents, like historical monographs, textbooks, and graphs.

Do these practice units one at a time or pick and choose examples that support your current history class—no matter which unit. Whichever approach you use, the remaining units are all about practice, so dig in and remember, the process is as easy as 1-2-3!

First-hand Private Accounts

Primary source documents, such as personal letters, diaries, and journals, can be some of the most useful historical evidence. These first-hand private accounts often represent the author's most sincere thoughts about an historical event or personality. Of course, since they are not usually intended for publication, private accounts are often difficult to find, and their discovery usually generates quite a bit of excitement among historians. This type of document also presents unique challenges for those attempting to analyze it.

Part 1: Personal Letters

Even famous and very public historical figures wrote private, personal letters. Historians often use these letters to discern an important character's innermost thoughts about historical events. Of course, most often, because these are private letters written to family or personal friends, they do not focus on important historical events *directly*.

Czar Nicholas II of Russia played a key role in the events that unfolded in the months just prior to the start of World War I. History books tell us that he signed a defensive alliance with France (and later England) against the German Empire.

The resulting Triple Entente provided for a two-front war
in the event that Germany's Kaiser Wilhelm chose to attack
either France in the west or Russia in the east. Despite
this geographical disadvantage, the Kaiser, allied with his
neighbors in Austria, decided to launch Germany into the
greatest war the world had ever seen. As a student of history,
you might wonder what could have inspired Wilhelm II to act
so rashly under these tense conditions. One interesting bit of
information is that Wilhelm of Germany, Nicholas of Russia,
and George of England were all grandsons of Queen Victoria
of England—they were first cousins. You might wonder how,
or *if*, this fact might have affected the course of events leading
to the Great War. Below is a personal letter from Kaiser
Wilhelm II of Germany to his cousin, Czar Nicholas II of
Russia.

Dearest Nicky

Many thanks to you dear Alix and the children for your
kind wishes and the lovely china pot which accompanied
them. Thank God I could spend my birthday in happiness
especially owing to the presence of dear Sophy and
Georgy who had come all the way from Athen [Athens]
to spend the day with me. I am most gratified that you
still keep pleasant recollections of the visit you paid us last
summer on the occasion of Sissy's wedding, and you may
be assured that we all most heartily reciprocate your kind
feelings and remembrance.

* * * *

With best love to Alix and the dear children believe me,
dearest Nicky Ever your devoted cousin and friend

Willy

**SOURCE: Wilhelm II, Kaiser of the German Empire, a letter
to his cousin, Nicholas II, Czar of Russia, Jan. 30, 1914**

Summarize

What might be a good summary of this letter?

The document focuses on the personal lives of Wilhelm and Nicholas and their families. Apparently, Nicholas sent Wilhelm a "china pot" for his birthday. It also indicates that Nicholas had visited Germany for a family wedding in 1913. Wilhelm signs as "cousin and friend."

Analyze

How might the document be useful in better understanding the months before the start of WWI?

The document really says nothing directly about state affairs or the impending crisis. It does seem, however, to demonstrate a friendliness between two of the opposing leaders that belies the tensions between their respective states throughout 1914.

Criticize

Besides the "china pot," might Wilhelm have had any other motivation to write this letter? How might his intentions help us to better understand the events leading to the war?

Although we cannot know for certain what Wilhelm may have intended with this letter, it may be reasonable to speculate that he was using his personal relationship with his cousin, the czar, to cajole Nicholas away from his Entente commitment. Some historians have suggested, in fact, that Wilhelm may have convinced himself that his cousin, "Nicky," would never actually follow through with any aggressive actions against Germany because of their personal relationship. This false sense of security may have led Wilhelm to act somewhat recklessly when he chose to support the Austrian claims on Serbia in August of that year.

Part 2: Secret Correspondences

Among other kinds of correspondence that historians may analyze for clues to understanding history are letters of a not-so-personal nature that were nonetheless never intended for public view. Included in this category might be secret official letters and other diplomatic correspondence—the "burn after reading" stuff. As has become evident from many examples—the Pentagon Papers and WikiLeaks are just two—many of these documents are never "burned" and no amount of classification by the government can keep all documents of this kind from the public eye. One such example comes from the American Civil War.

In the earliest days of the presidency of Abraham Lincoln, the United States was thrown into a war with itself that would determine the future of American liberty and democracy. In the first major engagement between the Union and the rebel Confederacy, the Battle of Bull Run, Lincoln's forces, under the command of an aging General Winfield Scott, were embarrassed and chased from the field by the upstart rebel army. Commander-in-Chief Lincoln, with no military experience beyond army private, was desperate to find a general who could lead the Union forces to victory as quickly as possible and avoid a protracted civil war that might invite European interference and threaten American security and autonomy. One prospective name that was rumored was that of General Giuseppe Garibaldi, leader of the Red Shirts whose successful invasion of the Kingdom of Two Sicilies had been halted by the politics of his king, Victor Emmanuel of Piedmont-Sardinia. In 1861, Garibaldi had "exiled" himself to the small island of Caprera, just off Sardinia. At that moment, a minor diplomat of the Buchanan administration sent a personal letter to Garibaldi to determine his interest in leading the Union army.

The papers report that you are going to the United States, to join the army of the North in the conflict of my country. If you do, the name of LaFayette will not surpass yours. There are thousands of Italians and Hungarians who will rush to your ranks, and there are thousands and tens of thousands of American citizens who will glory to be under the command of the "Washington of Italy." I would thank you to let me know if this is really your intention. If it be I will resign my position here as Consul and join you. . . .

Source: James W. Quiggle, American Consul in Antwerp in the Buchanan administration, unofficial letter to General Giuseppe Garibaldi, 8 June 1861

Summarize

What does the document say? What does it mean?

Quiggle says that he has heard that Garibaldi intends to lead the Union army, and that he may expect great support from Americans of every background. The author flatters Garibaldi, calling him the "Washington of Italy," and suggests that he would gladly quit his diplomatic post to join an army led by Garibaldi.

Analyze

Why might this document be important to our understanding of history?

The letter lends credence to the idea that Lincoln may have considered Garibaldi as an alternative to the available American generals for the leadership of the Union forces.

Criticize

How might the meaning or importance of this document have been influenced by the authorship, audience, intent, and historical context?

Since the source is cited as an "unofficial" letter, it is possible that Lincoln knew nothing about it, and so, even if Garibaldi was officially considered for the Union generalship, this contact could have been initiated independently by Quiggle. It is possible that Quiggle was about to be replaced by a new Lincoln appointee, and was making an attempt to retain some employment in the new administration by providing Lincoln with an introduction to a charismatic, internationally successful military leader. Additionally, since he was likely on his way out anyway, Quiggle's efforts were without risk, and his offer to quit his post was somewhat disingenuous.

Part 3: Journals and Diaries

Journals and diaries, similar to personal letters, often reveal a person's more guarded views. Also like letters, journals and diaries are sometimes written with the intent that they will be read by others. Whereas a personal diary may hold the author's deepest secrets, a journal intended for public eyes may be little more than propaganda. An example of a "diary" with questionable intent is the prison diary of General Hideki Tojo. Written during his imprisonment after the Japanese surrender of 1945, this journal was not simply an outlet for General Tojo's private thoughts, but may have served as preparation for his trial as well as an apologia for Japan's actions in the war.

Thus, England and the United States supported the Chungking [Chinese] government [of Chiang Kai-Shek] in every way, obstructed the peace between Japan and China that Japan desired, and thwarted Japan's efforts towards East Asian stability. During this period, in July 1939, the United States suddenly gave notice of the abrogation of the treaty of commerce [signed in 1911, its termination restricted the importation of essential raw materials] thereby threatening the existence of the Japanese people. At present, looking back coolly upon the past, I think that both nations have much to reflect upon.

1. Both China and Japan should have emptied their hearts of ill-will, calmly explained their true positions to each other, and reflecting deeply on the fact that they were the cornerstones of stability in East Asia, should have more bravely followed the path of direct peace negotiations.

2. Likewise, in dealing with the China problem, the British and American side, which had particularly strong interests in China, should have based its judgments about the origins of the problem on direct observation of the actual circumstances at the time. . . .

Note 1. As for the China Incident . . . it is necessary to consider the deeper origins: the exclusion and insult of Japan throughout the entire Chinese region, boycotts of Japanese goods, the infringement of rights and revenues, and violence against resident Japanese. The [Western] powers have had similar experiences with China, such as the exclusion of foreigners in 1899 and the anti-Christian Boxer Rebellion [1899 -1901].

Source: Hideki Tojo, Japanese General and Prime Minister, from his prison diary, 1945–1948

Summarize

What does the document say? What does it mean?

Tojo claims that the U.S. and England interfered in East Asian affairs without regard for the good of that region. He also states that Japan and China should have recognized their mutual interests and avoided conflict with each other. Throughout the document, Tojo makes clear that, in his view, America, England, and China all took actions that violated basic Japanese rights and threatened the well-being of the Japanese people.

Analyze

Why might this document be important to our understanding of history?

Tojo's diary is particularly important to understanding the history of World War II because it helps to shed light on the motivations of Japan's government and military. Taken at face value, Tojo's account of events leading to Japan's attack on Pearl Harbor seems to show several serious misunderstandings among the major parties involved. If Japan viewed the treatment of its people by Chinese officials as analogous to the treatment of foreigners in China during the Boxer Rebellion, the Japanese invasion of the Chinese mainland may appear to be more reasonable.

Criticize

How might the meaning or importance of this document have been influenced by the authorship, audience, intent, and historical context?

The document bears a distinctly defensive tone, and that seems to be somewhat incongruous with a private diary. Why would Tojo make excuses for his actions to himself? Many historians believe that this "diary" was actually written to help Tojo prepare for his own defense in his postwar trial. In that light, words that may have been interpreted as explaining misunderstood feelings might more accurately be viewed as "he said, she said" excuses.

You Try It: The Truman Letter

Directions: Now it's time for you to put the 3-step process to work. For the exercise below, read the document and follow the instructions for each task.

We have discovered the most terrible bomb in the history of the world. It may be the fire destruction prophesied in the Euphrates Valley Era, after Noah and his fabulous Ark. . . . Anyway we 'think' we have found the way to cause a disintegration of the atom. An experiment in the New Mexican desert was startling - to put it mildly. Thirteen pounds of the explosive caused the complete disintegration of a steel tower 60 feet high, created a crater 6 feet deep and 1,200 feet in diameter, knocked over a steel tower 1/2 mile away, and knocked men down 10,000 yards away. The explosion was visible for more than 200 miles and audible for 40 miles and more.

The weapon is to be used against Japan between now and August 10th. I have told the Sec. of War, Mr. Stimson, to use it so that military objectives and soldiers and sailors are the target and not women and children. Even if the Japs are savages, ruthless, merciless and fanatic, we as the leader of the world for the common welfare cannot drop this terrible bomb on the old capital or the new [Kyoto or Tokyo]. . . . He [Stimson] and I are in accord. The target will be a purely military one and we will issue a warning statement asking the Japs to surrender and save lives. I'm sure they will not do that, but we will have given them the chance. It is certainly a good thing for the world that Hitler's crowd or Stalin's did not discover this atomic bomb. It seems to be the most terrible thing ever discovered, but it can be made the most useful.

Source: Harry S. Truman, U.S. president, from his private diary, 25 July 1945

Summarize

Choose the best summary of the document from among the following:

A.   President Truman celebrates the U.S. discovery of the atomic bomb and plans to use it quickly as a weapon against Japan.

B.   President Truman believes the Japanese to be savage and ruthless, and deserving of the destruction brought on by the atomic bomb.

C.   The atomic bomb is so destructive that the U.S. is very lucky that Russia or Germany didn't discover it first.

D.   The Japanese will not surrender, so the U.S. will drop an atomic bomb on one of their military targets.

E.   President Truman and Secretary of War Stimson are in agreement that the U.S. should unleash the destructive forces of an atomic weapon on the Japanese.

Analyze

Analyze the document in terms of its significance for a thorough understanding of Truman's decision to drop the atomic bomb on Hiroshima. Write your response in your notebook or on a separate sheet of paper.

Criticize

Which information from the source line is probably most significant to an analysis of this document?

Answers and Explanations

Summarize

As noted in the introduction, a great technique for paraphrasing (or summarizing) is to read a paragraph, cover it with your hand, then try to write the main idea in a single short phrase. It is important that you read each paragraph only once and cover it before you write the main idea. If you fail to cover the words, you are very likely to excerpt pieces in your main idea statement. Because we are so accustomed to copy-and-paste "research" techniques, we often "lift" specific words from the page without even noticing. Additionally, rereading a paragraph before paraphrasing it creates a very bad habit of the mind. Your brain shuts down on the first read in anticipation of the second. Although reading only once will make the task seem much more difficult at first, the practice will help you to improve your critical reading skills in every subject.

In the first paragraph of the example above, President Truman writes of the surprising and awesome destructiveness of the atomic bomb, detailing the test results and comparing them with biblical catastrophes. The second paragraph is devoted to Truman's intention to use the bomb in Japan. Together, Truman expresses awe at the results of the Manhattan Project and describes his intention to utilize this new weapon on the Japanese as soon as possible—answer choice A. The other four choices address only the second paragraph, and are, therefore, variously too specific. Answer choice B "lifts" Truman's description of the Japanese as "savage" and "ruthless," then distorts his view that no amount of ruthlessness deserves the kind of destruction he expects from the atomic bomb. Answers C, D, and E are all accurate details from paragraph two, but none of them summarizes the paragraph or the document in its entirety.

Analyze

Any study of U.S. History will familiarize you with the U.S. decision to use atomic weapons against Japan in 1945. The results of the Manhattan Project are widely discussed in U.S. history books and popularized in several films, some of which are commonly used in school. Teachers of this time period often ask students to debate the ethics of dropping a bomb with such a destructive force on any enemy, and in that context, an understanding of President Truman's personal views might be enlightening. Based on this document, Truman seems to comprehend fully the awesome destruction that he is about to unleash on Japan. Since he says that this "terrible" weapon should not be used against a civilian target, it seems clear that he too has weighed the ethical questions of using the atomic bomb. Ultimately, however, he implies that he believes the Japanese will never surrender, and, therefore, the U.S. is justified in using this weapon against them in order to bring the war to a speedy conclusion.

Criticize

This source cites the author and his role, Harry S. Truman, U.S. president, the "title" of the work from which it was excerpted, "his private diary," and the date it was written. Knowing that these are the very words of President

Truman, we can assume that nothing has been "lost in translation," though certainly, without seeing the complete document, we may be missing some relevant context.

Since we might assume that someone besides Truman published the diary entries, we might also wonder if they were printed in their original form, edited for space or continuity, or even simply excerpted to make the editor's point. Without knowledge to confirm these speculations, it is probably best to assume that the words have the same meaning as in their original context.

The fact that these words come from Truman's private diary implies that they are his innermost thoughts, perhaps the ideas he cannot share with anyone else due to his integral role in this grave situation. Of course, one might also argue that presidential diaries are often later published, whether in the writer's lifetime or posthumously, so Truman may have written these words knowing fully that they would be read and analyzed by future generations.

If we assume the first scenario, then Truman seems to be trying to act as humanely as possible, given the horrors of war and the intransigence, as he sees it, of the enemy. On the other hand, if he expected his diary to be published for posterity, we could be reading little more than an excuse for killing millions of Japanese civilians. So, which analysis is correct? Who knows? You can only speculate and, given just this one document and a general understanding of the history of World War II, you cannot be expected to be very certain.

Remember that any critical analysis of a source must be "reasonable and relevant". It is reasonable to assume that a "private diary" is not intended for a wider audience, but it is also reasonable to suggest that a President of the United States, especially at such a crucial point in history, may expect that his diary will be published and analyzed for generations beyond his lifetime. In either case, if you have demonstrated why your speculation might matter to your original analysis of the document, it will be relevant.

Finally, the date, 25 July 1945, fewer than 10 days after the successful test in New Mexico and only two weeks before the U.S. would bomb Hiroshima, is an indication of just how quickly events were advancing at the end of the Pacific war. The president's decision to utilize a weapon that had been tested successfully only once just one month earlier, the results of which he only knew through telegraphed messages to the Potsdam delegation, could be characterized as rash or reckless.

Of course, Truman's haste might also speak to the gravity of the situation in the summer of 1945. When presented with a seemingly relentless enemy and mounting casualties after years of brutal warfare, the President of the United States might be justified in doing whatever he could to end the bloodshed.

So, which bit of source information is most significant to understanding Truman's decision? Probably the fact that this is from his private diary is most important, and the way you interpret that information— intended for publication or not— would certainly impact your analysis of the document.

Moving Forward

In the next unit, you will analyze first-hand documents that we know were intended for publication. Newspaper articles, memoirs, and speeches, for example, can offer their own insight into the course of historical events. Even though these documents are unique from those presented in Unit 1, if you follow the systematic approach of *Mastering Document Analysis*— Summarize, Analyze, Criticize— you will have no difficulty understanding their importance in the context of history.

First–hand
Public Accounts

When you text your friends, you probably tell them exactly what's on your mind without regard for style or grammar, and without fear of misinterpretation. You and your friends are close, so they will undoubtedly understand your meaning, and it is very unlikely that anyone except the recipient will ever read your text. Would you take the same approach toward a letter-to-the-editor or a college admissions essay? With these examples, you cannot control who will read your words or what meaning they might infer. You would likely spend a good deal of time revising and reshaping these more public documents. The difference between a text to a friend and a letter-to-the-editor is typical of the differences between first-hand *private* accounts and first-hand *public* accounts. Among the best examples of this latter document type are newspapers, memoirs, and speeches.

Part 1: Newspapers

A great source of historical information is the newspaper article. Newspapers have been around in one form or another almost since the invention of the printing press in the 1400s. Newspapers and their writers have spread new ideas, incited revolutions, and chronicled some of the most important events of the past few centuries. Unlike private documents, newspapers are intended for a broad audience, and their authors are often encouraged to write articles with particular audiences in mind. Writers for *Stars and Stripes*, the U.S. Army's newspaper, for instance, must write with the sensitivities of U.S. military personnel in mind. Any analysis of this type of document, therefore, must take into account its audience, intent, and historical context.

At the conclusion of the First World War, it was widely accepted among European leaders that Germany should bear the blame for starting the war as well as for employing many of the most barbarous tactics experienced by its participants. Despite Woodrow Wilson's call for a "just peace," the European leaders' interpretation of "justice" was often equivalent to "retribution." Germany was punished geographically and financially, and many historians suggest that the humiliation experienced by the German people post-Versailles Treaty was a major factor leading to the meteoric rise of Adolf Hitler and the National Socialists. First-hand accounts of the Paris Peace Conference negotiations that resulted in the Treaty of Versailles vary, often according to the writer's preconceptions about German guilt. One such account comes from an editorial printed in the Dutch daily business journal, *Algemeen Handelsblad*. Read the excerpt and follow along with the analysis below.

> The peace conditions imposed upon Germany are so hard, so humiliating, that even those who have the smallest expectation of a "peace of justice" are bound to be deeply disappointed.
>
> Has Germany actually deserved such a "peace"? Everybody knows how we condemned the crimes committed against humanity by Germany. Everybody

knows what we thought of the invasion of Belgium, the submarine war, the Zeppelin raids. ... This "peace" offered to Germany may differ in form from the one imposed upon conquered nations by the old Romans, but certainly not in essence.

This peace is a mockery of President Wilson's principles. Trusting to these, Germany accepted peace. That confidence has been betrayed in such a manner that we regard the present happenings as a deep humiliation, not only to all governments and nations concerned in this peace offer, but to all humanity.

SOURCE: editorial on the Treaty of Versailles from the the Dutch daily financial newspaper, *Algemeen Handelsblad,* **June 1919**

Summarize

Try to summarize this excerpt in a single sentence.

The Germans were wrong in the war, but the treaty is humiliating and unjust.

Analyze

How might this document help to assess the German perspective on the Treaty of Versailles?

The position taken in this news article seems to corroborate the German view. It might be useful in an essay that attacks the legitimacy of the Treaty of Versailles.

Criticize

Is there anything in the source line that might be relevant to an understanding of European views on the Treaty of Versailles?

It is easy to understand why the Germans felt wronged by the treaty terms, especially after they had expected Wilson's proposed Fourteen Points Plan. This editorial comes from a Dutch newspaper, however, so its corroboration is somewhat surprising given the popular opinion that "everyone" in Europe wanted to punish Germany. In light of this document, perhaps the German perspective on the Treaty of Versailles was at least somewhat justified.

Since the editorial is published in June 1919, in the same month that the treaty was signed, it might imply that the harsh terms were surprising to some outside the Peace Conference. Of course, given the fact that we have no knowledge of any prior editorials that may have appeared in this Dutch newspaper, it is also possible that this is simply the culmination of a series of analyses of the negotiations that resulted in the Versailles Treaty. Either interpretation could be justified.

Part 2: Memoirs

At first glance, a memoir might resemble a personal journal—just another example of the private ruminations of some famous personality. In fact, the two are often quite similar in terms of style and subject, but not always so in terms of audience and intent. Authors of memoirs generally intend for them to be published and read widely, so these documents, unlike their private counterparts, may not actually reflect the innermost feelings of their authors at all. Sometimes famous historical characters write their memoirs with the intent of justifying or rationalizing actions they took or decisions they made decades earlier. Of course, knowing this inherent bias can help us to make even more sense of memoir documents.

An example of a memoir that has been criticized for just this type of intent is *The Fog of War*, by Robert McNamara. As Secretary of Defense under Presidents Kennedy and Johnson, McNamara played an integral role in the administration's decisions regarding Cuba and Vietnam. In retrospect, many historians believe that he was the driving force behind the U.S. policy regarding the Vietnam conflict. More than 40 years after the fact, McNamara decided to release his thoughts on those decisions in the form of a documentary film. That film was then adapted into the printed memoir from which the following document is excerpted.

That's what I call empathy. We must try to put ourselves inside their skin and look at us through their eyes, just to understand the thoughts that lie behind their decisions and their actions. ... In the Cuban missile crisis, at the end, I think we did put ourselves in the skin of the Soviets. In the case of Vietnam, we didn't know them well enough to empathize. And there was total misunderstanding as a result. They believed that we had simply replaced the French as a colonial power, and we were seeking to subject South and North Vietnam to our colonial interests, which was absolutely absurd. And we, we saw Vietnam as an element of the Cold War. Not what they saw it as: a civil war.

Source: Robert McNamara, former Secretary of Defense in the Kennedy and Johnson administrations, from the documentary, *The Fog of War*, based on the memoir of Robert McNamara, *In Retrospect: The Tragedy and Lessons of Vietnam*, 1996

Summarize

What does the document say? What does it mean?

McNamara suggests that a thorough understanding of another nation's actions and decisions requires empathy, which he defines as standing inside the skin of the other. He says further that this is what the Kennedy administration did successfully in the Cuban missile crisis, but failed to do in the Vietnam conflict.

Analyze

Why might this document be important to our understanding of history?

Since U.S. involvement in Vietnam is still debated, this document seems to support arguments that are critical of the decisions of American officials in the Kennedy and Johnson administrations. It might also be useful in an analysis of other foreign policy decisions using McNamara's definition of empathy.

Criticize

How might the meaning or importance of this document have been influenced by the authorship, audience, intent, and historical context?

Despite its personal tone and introspective subject matter, *The Fog of War* was intended for public consumption. Given the intensity of the criticisms that have been leveled at Secretary McNamara during the 40 years since Vietnam, it might be reasonable to suggest that he intended this work as an apologia or rationale. Even if we reserve judgment of his intentions, we might also note that the year of publication, 2005, was a time of much controversy about U.S. foreign policy regarding Iraq. Since many twenty-first-century pundits compared Iraq with Vietnam, McNamara may have simply seen an opportunity to publish his thoughts on that earlier conflict. In either case, it would be a bad idea to interpret this document as McNamara's innermost feelings without mentioning the possibility of some ulterior motive. Given our analysis above, however, an attempt by McNamara to apologize or rationalize his earlier actions may make the document even stronger as evidence that American officials made poor decisions regarding Vietnam. Why would he apologize if he did not agree with his critics?

Part 3: Speeches

If intentions are important in document analysis, then speeches could be some of the most fascinating documents. Public speakers certainly intend for their ideas to affect a wide audience, and that audience is often well defined in the document. The intentions of the speaker, though still unknown with certainty, are often more transparent than those of writers whose audience and precise historical contexts are less well-known. Additionally, since famous historical characters were also often very public figures, examples of their speeches are sometimes ubiquitous. It is for all of these reasons that speeches must be included among the most important public documents.

An example from American history is a speech given by one of history's losers. Wendell Willkie was the Republican challenger to the two-time incumbent, Franklin Delano Roosevelt. Although Willkie garnered almost 45% of the popular votes, FDR won an unprecedented third term as president. Shortly after the results were announced, Willkie delivered the following speech in a radio broadcast to the nation.

It is a fundamental principle of the democratic system that the majority rules. The function of the minority, however, is equally fundamental. It is about the function of the minority— 22,000,000 people, nearly half our electorate, that I wish to talk to you tonight. ... A vital element in the balanced operation of democracy is a strong, alert and watchful opposition. That is our task for the next four years. We must constitute ourselves a vigorous, loyal and public-spirited opposition party. ... It has been suggested that in order to present a united front to a threatening world, the minority should now surrender its convictions and join the majority. This would mean that in the United States of America there would be only one dominant party—only one economic philosophy— only one political philosophy of life. This is a totalitarian idea—it is a slave idea—it must be rejected utterly. ... We, who stand ready to serve our country behind our Commander in Chief, nevertheless retain the right, and I will say the duty, to debate the course of our government. Ours is a two-party system. Should we ever permit one party to dominate our lives entirely, democracy would collapse and we would have dictatorship. Therefore, to you who have so sincerely given yourselves to this cause, which you chose me to lead, I say: "Your function during the next four years is that of the loyal opposition." ... It is your constitutional duty to debate the policies of this or any other Administration and to express yourselves freely and openly to those who represent you in your state and national government.

Source: Wendell L. Willkie, Republican candidate for the U.S. presidency, from a national radio address one week after he lost the election to Franklin Delano Roosevelt, 11 November 1940

Summarize

What does the document say? What does it mean?

Willkie makes the point that, although the United States is governed by majority rule, the minority has a vital role in governing as well. He says that the minority must remain committed to vocal opposition in order to avoid the problems of a single-party "dictatorship".

Analyze

Why might this document be important to our understanding of history?

Willkie's speech serves as evidence that, even during the four-term "reign" of FDR, the country sustained a strong and vocal opposition. It also demonstrates by its language the nation's opposition to totalitarianism and continued support of the democratic ideal. If a U.S. History essay asked students to "assess the electoral mandate for a continuation of New Deal policies evident in the election of FDR to an historic third term as president," this document could be used to demonstrate that Roosevelt's victory in 1940 may not have been a mandate at all.

Criticize

How might the meaning or importance of this document have been influenced by the authorship, audience, intent, and historical context?

Any "concession speech" may be expected to include words of reconciliation of the opposing parties as well as a nod toward the loyal opposition, but Willkie's speech might be extraordinary for several reasons. Students of American History may be aware that Wendell Willkie was a dark-horse candidate for the Republican Party in 1940. The frontrunners among the party elite were so divided, that the party chose a former Democrat as its candidate. Willkie was a staunch supporter of New Deal reform and relief programs, but disagreed with FDR's willingness to continue spending huge sums of federal money to achieve economic recovery. With this in mind, perhaps our assessment of the electoral mandate needs to be reevaluated. The voters in 1940 were faced with two visions of continuing the New Deal, so growing opposition to FDR's policies may be overstated by simply counting the votes. An alternative explanation for the closeness of the 1940 election could lay in the fact that one plank of Willkie's presidential platform was anti-isolationism in the face of WWII. It may be argued that American popular opinion, so entrenched in isolationism since WWI, might have been swinging in favor of U.S. participation in the war. In fact, U.S. History students may also know that Willkie later became a key figure in helping FDR to push for the Lend-Lease program. Wendell Willkie's speech might have been a reminder that, in times of crisis as well as in times of calm, the American government benefits from the active participation of its opposition.

You Try It: Robespierre, "On Political Morality" Speech

Directions: For the exercise below, read the document and follow the instructions for each task.

What is the goal toward which we are heading? The peaceful enjoyment of liberty and equality; the reign of that eternal justice whose laws have been inscribed, not in marble and stone, but in the hearts of all men, even in that of the slave who forgets them and in that of the tyrant who denies them. . . . We seek an order of things in which all the base and cruel passions are enchained, all the beneficent and generous passions are awakened by the laws; where ambition becomes the desire to merit glory and to serve our country; where distinctions are born only of equality itself; where the citizen is subject to the magistrate, the magistrate to the people, and the people to justice; where our country assures the well-being of each individual, and where each individual proudly enjoys our country's prosperity and glory; where every soul grows greater through the continual flow of republican sentiments, and by the need of deserving the esteem of a great people; where the arts are the adornments of the liberty which ennobles them and commerce the source of public wealth rather than solely the monstrous opulence of a few families....

What kind of government can realize these wonders? Only a democratic or republican government. ... But, in order to lay the foundations of democracy among us and to consolidate it, in order to arrive at the peaceful reign of constitutional laws, we must finish the war of liberty against tyranny and safely cross through the storms of the revolution: that is the goal of the revolutionary system which you have put in order. ... We must smother the internal and external enemies of the Republic or perish, in this situation, the first maxim of your policy ought to be to lead the people by reason and the people's enemies by terror.

If the mainspring of popular government in peacetime is virtue, amid revolution it is at the same time [both] virtue and terror: virtue, without which terror is fatal; terror, without which virtue is impotent. Terror is nothing but prompt, severe, inflexible justice; it is therefore an emanation of virtue. ... It has been said that terror was the mainspring of despotic government. Does your government, then, resemble a despotism? Yes, as the sword which glitters in the hands of liberty's heroes resembles the one with which tyranny's lackeys are armed. Let the despot govern his brutalized subjects by terror; he is right to do this, as a despot. Subdue liberty's enemies by terror, and you will be right, as founders of the Republic. The government of the revolution is the despotism of liberty against tyranny. Is force made only to protect crime?

Source: Maximilien Robespierre, "On Political Morality," from a speech delivered to the National Convention of France, 5 February 1794

Summarize

Without rereading the document, try to summarize it in a single sentence.

Analyze

Choose from the following the best analysis of the document in terms of the question, "To what extent were the decisions of Maximilien Robespierre rooted in the Enlightenment?"

A. Because Robespierre argues that the use of terror is a legitimate means to a republic of virtue, a concept espoused by Rousseau, Robespierre's decision to use terror seems to be rooted in Enlightenment thought.

B. Robespierre's decision to use terror is Machiavellian.

C. Terror violates man's natural right to life, therefore, it could never be rooted in the Enlightenment.

D.   Robespierre argues that terror is necessary to achieve a republic of virtue.

E.   Robespierre's decisions are directly connected to Enlightenment thought.

Criticize

How might the date of this document assist in a better understanding of its text?

Answers and Explanations

Summarize

At first, it may seem impossible to summarize such a lengthy document into a single sentence. In fact, Robespierre discusses several key ideas which almost certainly must be included in any summary. He outlines the goals of the French republic, explains why democracy is desirable, and finally explains the necessity of using terror to achieve the republic's goals. Some might argue that a sentence for each of these major ideas is absolutely necessary. A more efficient approach, however, might begin with Robespierre's primary purpose. What drove him to make this speech? The answer is that he wished to argue in favor of a democratic government's use of terror. The rest of the speech simply provides elements of his argument. A single-sentence summary could sound something like this:

Robespierre justifies the use of terror by a democratic government by connecting both the government and the terror to a common source— virtue.

Analyze

In order for the analysis to be useful, it must connect the document to the terms of the question. Choice A, in fact, connects Robespierre's argument to Rousseau's ideas and identifies those ideas as "Enlightenment thought," so this choice is a good analysis of the document. Choice B makes a valid point about the document: Robespierre essentially argues that his goal justifies his methods—a Machiavellian idea. Unfortunately, this answer choice fails to connect the document to the terms of the question and it mentions specifics of neither. Even though it is an attempt to reject the premise, it must explicitly discuss the document text and the question terms. If choice B had indicated what specifically was Machiavellian in the document and that Machiavelli was not an Enlightenment thinker, it would have been an acceptable analysis. Choice C has a similar problem, but here the statement fails to connect to "decisions of Robespierre." Choice D is merely a summary of the document with no connection to any of the question terms, and choice E addresses the terms of the question but says nothing of the specifics of this document. Choice A is the only one that explicitly connects the specifics of the document to the terms of the question, so it is the best overall analysis.

Criticize

According to the source line of the document, this speech was delivered to the French National Convention on "5 February 1794." Students of the French Revolution will probably remember that in the winter of 1793-94, Robespierre and the Committee of Public Safety were at the height of their power in the French republic. Additionally, by the opening months of 1794 there were several factions within the great Committee—among them, followers of Danton, Hebert, and Robespierre. Danton and Hebert would lose their heads by the end of March for their opposition. This speech could be viewed as an attempt by Robespierre to consolidate his own power and diminish that of his opponents on the committee. In this light, it would make sense for Robespierre to connect his decisions to the Enlightenment ideas on which the French Revolution was founded. Who among them would argue that liberty and equality—two of the great principles of the Revolution—were not justifiable goals? This critical analysis of the source lends even more credence to the position taken in the Analyze section above.

This exercise helps to illustrate the point that "criticize" does not have to mean "find bias." Too often, students assume that the only reason to critically analyze the source is to determine the reliability of the document. Although a critical analysis can find bias in the source of a document, more often, it simply helps us to better understand why the text might read as it does. As in this example, placing the document into its historical context may actually help to support the connection found between the document text and the question terms.

Moving Forward

In the next unit, you will analyze literary documents—poetry, music, fiction, and drama. This type of document is often difficult for students to analyze because the author may use symbolic language, but despite this apparent difficulty, if you follow the systematic approach that we have applied to first-hand documents in Units 2 and 3—Summarize, Analyze, Criticize—you will be able to place these unique documents into their historical contexts.

UNIT

4

Literary Documents

There are dozens, perhaps even hundreds, of literature textbooks that provide instruction for literary analysis. Students are directed to address plot, character, metaphor, allusion, symbolism, etc. Although historical analysis of literary documents may make use of some of these concepts, it is most important to remember that the task of historians is very different from that of literary critics. Our primary concern in analyzing literary documents is in determining their importance within the context of history. In the process, we need to consider what the words say, how they may have been important within the context of events of the day, and what may have influenced the author to write these particular words—we have to Summarize, Analyze, and Criticize.

Part 1: Poetry

Okay, poetry may not be quite as straightforward as a letter or newspaper article, but if you follow the basic steps of document analysis, it may not be as difficult as you might imagine. Although you may benefit from an understanding of form, imagery, metaphor, and symbolism, a simple analysis of the actual words and phrases can bear much fruit. Another factor that makes this process easier than it might be otherwise is the choice of poetry excerpts. Most history teachers use poetry to reinforce bigger historical trends or concepts, so the documents you are most likely to encounter will probably be a bit more literal than those you might see in a literature class. So, take off your "I Hate Poetry" hat and try applying the document analysis process to the following example.

The death and destruction of the First World War led many observers to conclude that life was not so certain as their leaders would have had them believe. Artists of the period turned to new forms and styles to reflect feelings of hopelessness, confusion, and despair. T.S. Eliot, an American-born poet who spent much of his life in England, wrote one of the most powerful poems of the period, *The Waste Land*. The poem utilizes many classical allusions and symbols, and Eliot is known to be quite difficult to understand, but try to apply the process developed in the previous units to analyze the following excerpt.

Unreal City,

Under the brown fog of a winter dawn,

A crowd flowed over London Bridge, so many,

I had not thought death had undone so many.

Sighs, short and infrequent, were exhaled,

And each man fixed his eyes before his feet.

SOURCE: from *The Waste Land*, T.S. Eliot, American-born poet living in England, 1922

Summarize

Try to summarize this excerpt in a single sentence.

There is a crowd of seemingly weary people (perhaps dead) walking across London Bridge.

Analyze

How might this document help us to better understand the impact of WWI on British society?

In six lines of poetry, Eliot creates a scene of walking dead that evokes feelings of despair and hopelessness. If his work reflects the general mood in post-WWI England, it helps to corroborate the disillusionment expressed by non-artists and embodied in the Lost Generation.

Criticize

How does the source line affect your interpretation of the text?

The title of the poem, "The Waste Land," immediately conjures images of barrenness and despair, which helps to support our analysis above. Additionally, the poem was printed in 1922, which would imply that Eliot penned the words during the war, or only shortly after it ended. We might assume that the images of war were still fresh in his mind and, therefore, his poem could be said to more accurately reflect the reality. Of course, if you happen to know that Eliot did not actually go to war, you may also argue that his perspective is one of an outsider—if the poem makes a statement about war. On the other hand, as a resident (and later citizen) of England during the war, Eliot was in a perfect position to witness and comment on the effects of the war on life in England.

Part 2: Music

Like poetry, music can be used to express often strong opinions about historical events. Of course, also like poetry, music is sometimes difficult to understand. Think of the lyrics to your favorite songs and try to imagine how the writer might have rewritten those words as a thesis essay. What if Bruno Mars had written like this: To the extent that her eyes are brighter than the stars and her hair falls perfectly all the time, she is perfect just the way she is; however, to the extent that she fails to acknowledge her own beauty, she is actually somewhat less than perfect. "Just the Way You Are" would probably not have been such a big hit, but you can see how the song argues this point.

A perfect example of a song with a point (several points actually) is "Over There," written by George M. Cohan at the start of America's involvement in World War One. The song expresses all the hope, determination, and confidence of pre-war America. Read the following excerpt from the chorus and try to answer the questions that follow.

Over there, over there,
Send the word, send the word over there –
That the Yanks are coming,
The Yanks are coming,
The drums rum-tumming
Ev'rywhere.
So prepare, say a pray'r,
Send the word, send the word to beware.
We'll be over, we're coming over,
And we won't come back till it's over
Over there.

SOURCE: from "Over There," George M. Cohan, American lyricist, 1917

Summarize

Summarize the chorus in a single sentence.

Tell everyone that the Americans are coming to save the day.

Analyze

What does this tell us about America's understanding of the war in Europe?

The bravado of this chorus implies that the Americans see themselves as strong enough in 1917 to end a war that has stalemated the European powers for three years. In fact, "say the word to beware" seems to imply that the "bad guys" are unprepared for the strength of the Americans. The chorus is almost saying, "We don't care who started this fight—we are going to finish it, so look out!" If this interpretation is accurate, the Americans, like the Europeans in 1914, may have underestimated the difficulty of winning this war.

Criticize

Does the source line add anything to our analysis?

Most likely you will know little, if anything, about George M. Cohan, so authorship probably adds nothing to your critical analysis. We might say that because the song was written in 1917, the year that we declared war on Germany, Cohan's experience and understanding of the Great War was likely limited to reports in American newspapers. Since he probably had no firsthand knowledge of the fighting conditions or the difficulties faced by the Allies since 1914, his view of America's impact on the war might be an expression of jingoism (a popular sentiment near the turn of the century) rather than a realistic assessment of our prospects.

Part 3: Fiction

Fiction may seem an odd choice for historical document analysis. After all, it isn't real—it's fiction. Often, however, fiction, like poetry, is an author's statement about reality. Historical fiction, in particular, may create a fictitious plot within an historically accurate setting, so the setting helps us to better understand the period. Even fiction outside the historical realm can be allegorical and, therefore, argue quite persuasively for a particular point of view about actual events and people, without actually mentioning these events and people.

A good example of historical fiction is a recent book by Mary Ann Shaffer and Annie Barrows (if you were an Ivy & Bean fan as a kid, it's that Annie Barrows), *The Guernsey Literary and Potato Peel Pie Society*. The title is a mouthful, but the book tells an engaging story about a group of British citizens in the Nazi-occupied Channel Islands. Many people know nothing at all about this occupation, but it's real and Barrows does a great job bringing it to life in this little historical fiction. The story is told through correspondence between an author and several Guernsey citizens after the war. The following excerpt tells of a young woman who has recently returned from a Nazi prison camp in northern Germany.

She will not tell you how sick she has been, but I will. In the few days before the Russians arrived at Ravensbrück, those filthy Nazis ordered anyone who could walk to leave. Opened the gates and turned them loose upon the devastated countryside. "Go," they ordered. "Go— find any Allied troops that you can."

They left those exhausted, starving women to walk miles without any food or water. There were not even any gleanings [crop remnants left after harvest] left in the fields they walked past. Was it any wonder their walk became a death march? Hundreds of the women died on the road.

After several days, Remy's legs and body were so swollen with famine edema [swelling due to long-term starvation], she could not continue to walk. So she just laid herself down in the road to die. Fortunately, a company of American soldiers found her. ...

SOURCE: Sister Cecile Touvier, a nurse caring for Remy Giraud in *The Guernsey Literary and Potato Peel Pie Society* (a fiction published in 2008), from a letter dated 14 June 1946.

Summarize

What does the document say? What does it mean?

Sister Touvier describes Remy Giraud's ordeal upon being released from the Nazi camp, Ravensbrück. She says that Remy was part of a "death march" in which hundreds of women perished of starvation, and that Remy might have died as well, if she had not been discovered by passing American soldiers.

Analyze

Why might this document be important to our understanding of the history of WWII?

Although the characters are fictitious, the events described in this excerpt actually occurred. The Nazis released thousands of women from the Ravensbrück prison camp as the Russians approached in 1945, and hundreds of these women died on the road. This document adds detail to the event and brings to life this horrible episode in the war.

Criticize

How might the meaning or importance of this document have been influenced by the authorship, audience, intent, and historical context?

First the obvious— it's a fiction! Even if the story is based on an actual event, the author's embellishments may have distorted the event considerably. Despite that, the fact that the book was written more than 50 years after the war may argue for greater circumspection on the part of the author. She has thousands of resources available to her, each with its own analysis of the Nazi effort. In addition to describing the Nazis as "filthy," which probably corroborates the general opinion today, the author puts these words in the mouth a nun.

Part 4: Drama

Drama, like fiction, may be more or less realistic, but our perception of the play as strictly fiction may be unique to this era. In ancient Greece, for instance, playwrights were often also historians. They brought to life the true stories and actual heroes and villains of history. The same may be said largely of Renaissance playwrights. William Shakespeare, probably the most famous of them, wrote many plays about famous figures from history. One example of Shakespeare's more historical dramas is *Julius Caesar*. Based on the renewed interest in the classics common in the Renaissance, Shakespeare created a drama to portray the rise and fall of one of the greatest heroes of ancient history. Read the following excerpt and think about what it says, not just about ancient Rome, but also about Elizabethan England.

'Tis a common proof,

That lowliness is young ambition's ladder,

Whereto the climber-upward turns his face;

But when he once attains the upmost round,

He then unto the ladder turns his back,

Looks in the clouds, scorning the base degrees

By which he did ascend.

SOURCE: Marcus Brutus, speaking of Julius Caesar and his ascendency, from Act 2, Scene 1 of *Julius Caesar*, by William Shakespeare, circa 1600.

Summarize

What does the document say? What does it mean?

Basically, Brutus is saying that a young man's ambition is built on the lowly conditions of his life, but that once he achieves his goals, he forgets about those he left behind.

Analyze

Why might this document be important to our understanding of ancient Rome? Why might it be important to our understanding of Elizabethan England?

Julius Caesar was, indeed, assassinated because those around him thought he had become too powerful. Brutus explains how power can corrupt those who achieve it. If these words are representative of the general view of the Roman Senate in 44 BC, then Caesar, well-known for ignoring tradition and clearly attempting to usurp the traditional power of the Senate, may have created an environment within which his assassination was almost inevitable. Additionally, since we know that these lines were actually written by Shakespeare in the 16th century, the document may be evidence of the humanist perspective on power as well. Perhaps Shakespeare is cautioning Renaissance monarchs against forgetting from whence they came. His advice, had it been heeded by the Stuart kings, might well have saved the head of Charles I.

Criticize

Does the source line add anything to our analysis?

Most of what we might say regarding the source information has been discussed in our analysis. The three steps often overlap. In fact, when you have mastered your document analysis skills, your analyses will often interweave the summary, analysis, and critique. One additional note about this document's source line, however, is that the play was written near the year 1600, at the end of the reign of Queen Elizabeth I. Elizabeth is widely acknowledged as the greatest monarch of England, and her reign prepared the way for the divine right "absolutism" of the Stuart kings. She died in 1603 and, by then, her critics had enough ammunition to suggest that Elizabeth may have become too powerful. This could lend further credence to our contention that Shakespeare was cautioning future monarchs to tread more lightly on those beneath them.

You Try It: **Hector's Speech,** *The Iliad*

Directions: For the exercise below, read the document and follow the instructions for each task that follows.

> He who among you finds by spear thrown or spear thrust his death and destiny, let him die. He has no dishonor when he dies defending his country, for then his wife shall be saved and his children afterwards, and his house and property shall not be damaged, if the Achaeans must go away with their ships to the beloved land of their fathers.
>
> **Source: Hector, speaking to his troops before battle, from** *The Iliad* **by Homer, circa 800 BC**

Summarize

Summarize the document in a single sentence.

Analyze

Choose from the following the best analysis of the document in terms of the question, "In what ways did the location of the Trojan War impact the course of the battle?"

A.   Hector tells his men to die with honor for their country.

B.   Hector's troops may fight with more passion because he reminds them that the war is in Troy, so they are defending their homeland.

C. The war takes place on Trojan soil.

D. Hector tells his men that the Achaeans are invaders.

E. There is no dishonor in dying for your country.

Criticize

How might the date of this document help to assess our analysis of the text?

Answers and Explanations

Summarize

Again, use the technique introduced in Unit 1— read the document once, cover it with your hand, and then write your summary statement. Unlike the Robespierre piece in Unit 3, this one is not long at all. In fact, if you were even marginally successful with the practice documents in the first two units of this book, I'll bet this one is a piece of cake. As you may already know, *The Iliad* is a story about the Trojan War, and you need only have seen the movie, *Troy*, to know that two of the main characters are the rival commanders, Hector and Achilles. In this excerpt, Hector prepares his men for battle. Your summary might read something like this:

Hector tells his men that there is great honor in dying to save their families.

Analyze

This analysis must connect the document summary to the terms of the question, the location of the Trojan War and the course of the battle. Answer choice A simply restates the summary—it is part of the answer but fails to address the terms of the question. Choice C states a fact which can be inferred from the document, but like A, it fails to address the terms of the question. Answer D is the documentary evidence that leads to the inference in choice C, but still does not address the terms of the question. Answer choice E restates a part of the document, but again, fails to address the tasks and terms. Answer B is the correct answer. It connects Hector's appeal to his troops to the location of the war and the possible course of the battle.

Criticize

From the source line, we learn that Homer wrote *The Iliad* around 800 BC. A study of ancient history places the Trojan War at about 1200 BC—400 years earlier. Even though you probably already knew that Homer wrote the poem long after the actual event, the source line of this document drives home the point that, despite Homer's inclusion of dialogue, this is not a firsthand account. There was no way for Homer to know for certain who said what, or even who was there. Tradition holds that Homer wrote *The Iliad* based on a long oral history of the great battle, but you only need to have played "Telephone" one time to know that oral history can be distorted over the long term. Although the document seems to support the argument that the defenders will fight more vigorously on their homeland, since the words are not likely accurate, the document may do nothing to support this thesis. On the other hand, even if Hector never said these words, Homer's inclusion of this speech in his epic poem could be an indication of the fighting spirit of the defending Trojans as passed down through four centuries of oral tradition.

Moving Forward

Just remember when analyzing literary documents that your primary concern is in determining their importance within the context of history—a crucial difference from the focus you've been taught in your English classes.

In the next unit, you will analyze visual documents—paintings, photographs, and cartoons. This type of document is usually difficult for students to analyze because, without words, there seems to be no "message" to summarize, but fear not—the three-step approach you have mastered in the preceding units of this book can be used just as effectively with visual documents. Press on!

UNIT
5

Visual Documents

Visual documents are some of the most intimidating documents to analyze. After all, there are no words— how are we supposed to know what the author was trying to say? Paintings, photographs, and cartoons, however, can be even more telling than written documents—a picture is worth a thousand words. In this unit, you will learn to adapt *Mastering Document Analysis*'s three-step process—Summarize, Analyze, Criticize—to visual documents.

Summarizing a visual document involves creating a written statement that accurately describes the image. This serves at least two purposes: it forces you to look carefully at the details of the image, and it clarifies your perception of the image for your reader— because not everyone will see the same details in the same image. Once this "summary" is complete, you will have a written document. Then the Analyze and Criticize steps will be applied exactly as they have been in the previous three units. With this systematic approach, you will begin to see visual documents as valuable and very understandable sources of historical evidence.

Part 1: Paintings and Drawings

We begin with paintings and drawings because this form of
visual expression has been around since the caves of Lascaux.
For literally millennia, people have attempted to tell stories
and state opinions using colors and sketch. Although these
images were often meant to reflect reality as it actually was,
the scene first had to be processed and translated through the
artist's perception, and this has a definite impact on the end
result. The first example is filled with details, so look carefully
and follow the three-step process—Summarize, Analyze,
Criticize.

One of the bloodiest events in early modern Europe (and there
were many bloody events) was the St. Bartholomew's Day
Massacre. Beginning on the feast day for which it is named
and continuing for several weeks, the event involved mobs of
French Catholics killing French Huguenots, first in Paris and
then throughout the countryside. Estimates of the death toll
among the Protestants vary up to about 30,000; more extreme
historians have suggested as many as 100,000 may have
died. Historians are also divided on the causes and culprits
of the massacre. Some give evidence of a premeditated plot
organized by the queen, Catherine de Medici, and implicating
a variety of co-conspirators, including Philip II of Spain and
even the Pope. Because the animosity between Catholics and
Protestants in France had been developed over decades of
intense and bloody religious wars, and since these are the
authors of the many accounts of the massacre, first-hand
reports can be found to support almost any historical analysis.
With this in mind, look at the following painting of the event
and answer the questions that follow it.

SOURCE: *St. Bartholomew's Day Massacre* by François Dubois, a Huguenot painter born 1529 in Picardy, date of painting unknown

Summarize

Describe what you see in this image.

The painting shows a battle scene. There are people being killed in the street, thrown from windows, and dragged from a castle. The victims appear to be unarmed but those doing the killing use a variety of pikes, clubs, sabers, and muskets. The perpetrators of the massacre are a mixture of what appear to be soldiers, cavalrymen, and commoners. There is a group of three men in the street that appear from their attire to be nobility and they seem to be directing some of the action before them. Additionally, there are two separate groups of soldiers in the background who seem to be breaking into buildings or dragging people from the buildings. In the left part of the background there is an individual dressed in a robe standing over a pile of dead bodies.

Analyze

How might this document help us to better understand the causes of the St. Bartholomew's Day Massacre?

The painting shows all manner of inhumanity committed as part of the attack on the Huguenots. The presence of soldiers might support political causes, possibly implicating the royal family. Some have suggested that the robed person on the left is Catherine de Medici. If so, her inclusion in the scene is certainly an indication of where Dubois places blame. If the robed individual is seen as a priest, his inclusion could help to support the argument that the Catholic Church assisted, or at least supported, the killers. Of course, since it is difficult to determine exactly what this person is doing, it could be argued that a priest might be administering last rites to the dead, perhaps in sympathy to their plight. The three noblemen seem to be directly in league with the soldiers, so perhaps their presence supports an argument implying class warfare. Since, as many historians point out, French Huguenots were among the wealthiest citizens, it is not difficult to imagine the nobility supporting the massacre to insure their own privilege against the up-and-coming Huguenots.

Criticize

How might the source line affect our analysis?

Because Dubois was a Huguenot painter, it could be said that he may have depicted the Catholics more harshly than they deserved because of his relation to those massacred. Since it is somewhat difficult to imagine weeks of struggle in which the targets would fail to take arms against their attackers, Dubois may have enhanced the viewer's sympathy for the Huguenots by portraying them as unarmed, even if that was not true. Of course, it might also be noted that Dubois was born in 1529, and, although the date of the painting is unknown, it would be reasonable to suggest that he may have witnessed the 1572 massacre first-hand. In fact, he probably did not witness the event, but you might also use the date to point out that this painting must have been created within 50 years of the actual occurrence since it is unlikely that Dubois lived beyond 1622. In fact, if you happened to know that he died in 1584, you could say that the image was created within ten years of the massacre—so still very fresh in the mind of the artist.

Part 2: Photographs

Paintings and photographs are very much alike— they represent an artist's view of a particular visual scene. Paintings, however, can alter reality in big ways— look at some of Picasso's works. In the previous section of this unit, we suggested that Dubois, a Huguenot painter, might have portrayed the Protestants killed in the St. Bartholomew's Day Massacre as unarmed victims in order to evoke sympathy in the viewer. Although new technology has made it easier to alter photographs as well, historically, photos have been an exact duplicate of whatever was in front of the artist's camera. Of course, even from the earliest days of photojournalism, photographers have "staged" scenes to produce a desired reaction. Matthew Brady, the famous photographer who

chronicled the American Civil War actually moved bodies on
the battlefield to create the scenes he wanted to portray.

Below is a photo of Mahatma Gandhi enroute to the sea to
protest the British Salt Tax. Follow the same process that you
used above and try to determine the historical importance of
this document.

**SOURCE: Photo of Indian spiritual leader, Mahatma
Gandhi, enroute to breaking the Salt Laws at the end of his
long march to inaugurate the Civil Disobedience campaign,
1930**

Summarize

What do you see in the photograph?

There are seven people in the frame of the photo, including Gandhi, who is pictured holding a long stick. The woman next to Gandhi at the front of the group is holding something that appears to be a loop of fabric. Additionally, parts of other people can be seen at the edges of the frame, possibly cropped out of the photo—either at the time it was taken or later.

Analyze

What does this photo tell about the Indian independence movement?

Since Gandhi is at the front of the group, he appears to be their leader. If this group is just a small representation of a larger group as appears to be the case from looking at the edges of the frame, then Gandhi's movement may be said to be very popular. Everyone in the photo appears to be calm and peaceful and no one seems to have any sort of a weapon (if Gandhi's stick is assumed to be for walking), and this would seem to corroborate what most people know about Gandhi and his use of civil disobedience.

Criticize

Does the source line add anything to our analysis?

It is difficult to say much about the motives of the photographer without further notes in the citation. One might argue, however, that either the photographer or a later editor may have cropped the photo to imply that the Salt March involved only a small group of followers (there were actually 78 in total).

Part 3: Cartoons

Cartoons are among the most often used historical visual documents. They are also some of the easiest to analyze because the artist usually creates the cartoon to make an argument and often includes words to help make the thesis clearer to the viewer. This type of visual document was used as political commentary in the form of graffiti sketched on buildings in the Roman Empire, and the tradition continued throughout the history of Europe and the modern world. One of the most famous political cartoonists in America was Thomas Nast. His images published in Harper's Weekly Magazine have become a staple of U.S. History classes.

In the 1860s, the United States was embroiled in a civil war that tore the country apart. Although the Union won the war and the fighting ended in 1865, the postwar political disputes were almost as vicious as the battles in the field. Andrew Johnson had succeeded to the presidency upon Lincoln's assassination, but his administration chose to push reconstruction in a new direction. Many people, Nast among them, accused Johnson of usurping too much power and disregarding the will of the people. Look at the following cartoon and try to answer the questions that follow.

SOURCE: Thomas Nast, American political cartoonist, in *Harper's Weekly*, 20 April 1867

Summarize

What do you see in the picture?

Nast has portrayed Johnson leaning back in a chair with his feet on a table, while Seward, in a dress, rubs his head. Johnson looks at his own image in a mirror and sees a crown on his head. On the wall hang two pictures: one of two people (possibly Eskimos) that says "One of the Advantages" and another of the "Map of the Russian Fairyland" that says "Only $7,000,000 in gold." The caption of the cartoon reads: "The Big Thing." Old Mother Seward. "I'll rub some of this on his sore spot; it may soothe him a little."

Analyze

How might this document help in an analysis of the popularity of the Johnson administration?

Johnson's image in the mirror clearly implies that he sees himself as a king, perhaps above and detached from the citizenry. Since "Mother Seward" is rubbing a salve on his head, we can assume that Johnson is feeling ill, maybe implying that things are not going well for him. In fact, students of American history may already know that by mid-1867, Johnson had already broken with the moderates in Congress and squared off against the radicals, vetoing the Freedmen's Bill and the Civil Rights Bill. Both of these bills were overridden by his congressional opponents, so he seems to be not-so-popular on Capitol Hill. Additionally, the "salve" that Seward is using to make Johnson feel better is Alaska! Even if you were paying very little attention in U.S. History, you probably remember Seward's Folly. The pictures on the wall seem to show Nast's disapproval of the Alaska deal, and this document could be used as evidence of a popular view in opposition to Seward's purchase.

Criticize

Is there anything in the source line that might impact our analysis?

In this document, only the date is very helpful. As stated in the analysis, April 1867 is just after two major legislative defeats and a very unpopular land deal with Russia.

You Try It: Strothmann War Bonds Poster

Directions: For the exercise below, study the visual document and follow the instructions for each task.

SOURCE: Frederick Strothmann, U.S. poster for war bonds campaign, 1918

Summarize

Summarize the image.

Analyze

Choose from the following the best analysis of the document in terms of the question, "In what ways was propaganda used against Germany in WWI?"

A. The German soldier is pictured with blood on his hands.

B. Germany has already killed several Americans before the U.S. entered the war and they may be threatening our borders next.

C. German citizens were brainwashed with the Kaiser's propaganda, and now it was our turn to use propaganda against the Huns.

D. Propaganda was used by the Americans to gain popular support for war.

E. In U.S. propaganda posters, Americans are inspired to buy bonds by the portrayal of German soldiers as Huns (Attila, et al.) and pictured threatening us from just across the water.

Criticize

How might the date of this document help to assess our analysis of the text?

Answers and Explanations

Summarize

A very menacing giant wearing the German uniform is looking across the water from the smoking ruins of a city. He has blood on his fingers and a bloody bayonet in his hand. The poster reads: Beat back the Hun with Liberty Bonds.

Analyze

This analysis must connect the document summary to the tasks and terms of the question: "In what ways," "propaganda," and "Germany in WWI." Answer choice A is nothing more than a partial description of the image. Answer B, though perhaps true, is generally unrelated to the document, and so fails to connect. Answer choice C is a rant and not related to the document or the terms of the question. Answer choice D succinctly states one of the "ways" that Americans used propaganda against Germany in WWI, but fails to mention anything directly connected with the document. It is little better than A in terms of analysis that connects the document to the question terms. Choice E connects the document summary to the tasks and terms by noting that the image is a U.S. propaganda poster meant to inspire financial support for the war and that it portrays the Germans as barbarians who want to kill us. Choice E is the correct answer.

Criticize

Because the document is dated 1918, we can assume that the U.S. is already fighting in Europe. Students of American, World, or European history will remember that the U.S. entered the war in 1917. In fact, U.S. History students may also remember that Woodrow Wilson was

reelected in 1916 on the slogan "He kept us out of war."
We might infer from this fact that America was not entirely
prepared to fight in 1917, and so may still have needed
financial and popular support for the war effort in 1918.
Propaganda artists needed to generate as much emotion
as possible with their posters. Only if Americans felt an
immediate threat could the government depend on their
support.

Moving Forward

I hope this unit has helped to demystify visual documents.
Paintings, photographs, and cartoons can serve as a wealth
of historical evidence if you just apply the 3-step process of
Mastering Document Analysis – Summarize, Analyze, Criticize.

Our final unit addresses a few other document types —
Secondary Sources and Data Displays. You've probably
already learned the difference between primary and secondary
sources, but even beyond their definitions, the two differ
in terms of how you should incorporate them into your
understanding of history. But don't worry, just Summarize,
Analyze, Criticize — and be happy!

Other Document Types

When I was a kid, my family had an old set of *Funk & Wagnalls* encyclopedias. They were dull and grey, but if you wanted to know about something—as long as that something was pre-1950—the *Funk & Wagnalls* had the answer. I was a geek, so these were my favorite books. Then when I was 10, my parents bought me a set of *World Books*. I still remember opening them up and putting them in alphabetical order on my bookshelf. They had that "new book" smell—part paper, part leather, part glue. The cover of each book was a creamy pebbled leather with a smooth brown band accented by thin gold inlay, and when you stood all 24 volumes side-by-side on a shelf, they looked like a solid block of shimmering wisdom. They were beautiful! If my friends came to visit, they'd get a tour of my new *World Books*. (In retrospect, I wonder if that's why I didn't have too many friends.) I spent hours with those volumes. I'd pull down Volume 13, the M volume, and look at the bright color pictures of the moon and read how it was just 239,000 miles from Earth—it didn't seem so far. Armed with my new *World Book* encyclopedias, I dreamed of joining Neil Armstrong on his next visit.

Why was I so enamored with volumes of reference books that had the fascinating writing style of history textbooks?

It was because I was always curious about the world, and encyclopedias were the one place you could go to find information about almost anything! Today we have a love-hate relationship with encyclopedias. For one thing, there's Wikipedia—everything you ever wanted to know and were willing to ask random people on the internet. Then there's the internet itself. Through your school media center, you likely have instant access to reliable databases filled with the work of professional historians whenever you decide to fire up your smartphone. Because of this instant access, your teachers may have told you that you should get your information from better sources than just encyclopedias. Back in the day, we didn't have that sort of access. If I wanted an answer sometime before I could get to a library, I needed an encyclopedia.

Although we have discussed many different document types in the preceding units, encyclopedias are among the few remaining resources you will likely see in your study of history. The final few we will discuss are historical monographs, biographies, history textbooks, encyclopedias, charts, and graphs. Historical monographs are books about specific topics in history. They are secondary source documents because they are typically written long after the events they describe, and generally their authors are attempting to support an original thesis based on an analysis of several primary sources. Biographies are variations on this type of document. Tertiary sources are reference books based on the information taken from primary and secondary source authors, and they include history textbooks and encyclopedias. Finally, although raw data is considered a primary source, charts and graphs created from those data sets are secondary sources. Each of these other document types presents its own unique qualities and challenges, but in every case, they can be used to further your understanding of history—if you just Summarize, Analyze, and Criticize.

Part 1: Monographs

Just weeks after the Japanese attacked Pearl Harbor, British Prime Minister Winston Churchill visited the White House to begin planning for the United States' entry into the Second World War. During that visit, President Roosevelt accidentally entered Churchill's room as he emerged from his bath—stark naked. The Prime Minister allegedly responded by quipping that he had "nothing to hide from the President of the United States." This anecdote comes from *Churchill by Himself: The Life, Times and Opinions of Winston Churchill in His Own Words* by Richard M. Langworth.

Despite what you may have been told, history can be very entertaining. Walk through any bookstore (if you can still find one anymore) and you will see entire sections of the store dedicated to historical monographs and biographies—many that are national bestsellers! Like all the document types we have explored so far, monographs, biographies, and scholarly articles have much to add to our understanding of history, while providing fascinating insights into our search for the past.

One example of the value of the monograph in the study of history is in an interesting and engaging book, *City of Fortune: How Venice Ruled the Seas*, by Roger Crowley. In it, Crowley details the rise of Venice as a major sea power and a hub of commerce in the Mediterranean Sea. Read the following excerpt and apply the 3-step process to analyze the document.

What drove them [the Venetians] on were the possible returns, the "insatiable thirst for wealth" that baffled the scholarly Petrarch so much. At Tana [a Venetian trading city on the northern coast of the Black Sea] they acquired both the portable, lightweight, high-value luxury items of the farthest Orient and the bulk commodities and foodstuffs of the steppe hinterland: precious stones and silk from China and the Caspian Sea; furs and skins, sweet-smelling beeswax and honey from the glades of Russian forests; wood, salt, and grain, and dried or salted fish in infinite varieties from the Sea of Azov. In return, they shipped back the manufactured goods of a developing industrial Europe....

There was one other highly profitable item in which the Venetian merchants came to deal, although its business was always outstripped by the Genoese. Both Kaffa [Black Sea port controlled by Genoa] and Tana were active centers of slave trading. The Mongols raided the interior for "Russians, Mingrelians, Caucasians, Circassians, Bulgarians, Armenians, and diverse other people of the Christian world." The qualities of the ethnic groups were carefully distinguished—different peoples had different merits. ... Generally slaves were sold young—boys in their teens (to get the most work out of them); the girls, a little older. Some were shipped to Venice as domestic and sexual servants; others, to Crete in conditions of plantation slavery.... Or they were sold on in an illicit trade, expressly forbidden by the pope, as military slaves to the Mamluk Islamic armies of Egypt.

SOURCE: Roger Crowley, historian, in his book *City of Fortune: How Venice Ruled the Seas*, 2011

Summarize

What does the document say about the Venetians?

The document clearly portrays the Venetians as merchants seeking a profit at every turn. According to the author, they traded everything from luxury goods, to food, to slaves—all for economic gain.

Analyze

Analyze the document in terms of its significance for a better understanding of the role of Venice in world history.

You may have learned that Venice was a medieval center of trade, and this document supports that contention. Did you also know that, at the time of the Crusades, the Venetians had the strongest navy in the Mediterranean and that they actually used that navy to transport Crusader armies to the Holy Lands? In fact, when, in the Fourth Crusade, the Crusaders failed to compensate Venice for its ships, the Venetians sacked Constantinople to gain an edge over the Byzantines in the Black Sea trade. These actions seem to support Crowley's argument.

Criticize

Is there anything in the source line that might impact our analysis?

If you knew Roger Crowley, you would know that he is a kind-hearted historian who has conducted years of research into the events of medieval Mediterranean Sea powers. Unfortunately, you probably don't know anything about Roger Crowley, so you have only the information in the source line: he's a historian who has authored a book about Venice. Given the subtitle, *How Venice Ruled the Seas*, it is likely that the author has analyzed a variety of causes for Venetian success. If that is the case, and if this excerpt is representative of his overall thesis, then we can conclude that Venice was interested in profit above all else.

Part 2: Biographies

A biography is a special kind of monograph. Historians who produce these often-massive recountings of particular historical figures sometimes spend their entire careers researching. They immerse themselves in the time period, reading thousands of letters and other eyewitness accounts, in an attempt to understand their subjects as deeply and intimately as possible. The best examples tell a vivid story of one life, while simultaneously opening a window into a time and place within which that life had meaning.

One very popular biographer, Carolly Erickson, wrote several books about the Tudors of sixteenth-century England. You may remember that Mary Tudor was the oldest daughter and first-born of Henry VIII, notorious for discarding wives that proved unable to provide him a male heir. When Mary's mother, Catherine of Aragon, was divorced by Henry, mother and daughter were banished from the court. Influenced by only her mother and her mother's Catholic advisors, Mary grew up to be a staunch Catholic, who blamed Henry and his Protestant supporters for her royal humiliation. Of course, Mary eventually assumed the throne as Queen and proceeded to reestablish the Catholic Church as the central religious institution in England. Her efforts to eliminate the Protestant opposition led to her infamous nickname, Bloody Mary. Erickson's work on Mary Tudor, *Bloody Mary*, confronts her subject's brutal reputation head-on. Read the following excerpt, and analyze it in terms of the question, "To what extent did Mary Tudor deserve her reputation?"

The ballads that did most damage to the queen's repute were those that glorified the Protestant martyrs. Ballad-makers wove the names of the seventy-five men and women burned as heretics during 1555 into songs glorifying their heroism and blackening the clergy who burned them. The "Ballad of John Careless" was sung wherever Protestants gathered, and in many places where the Spaniards were feared and the queen's policies despised. Another song told the story of a woman condemned to the stake who gave birth to a child as she suffered in the flames; the blameless child was thrown into the fire to die with its mother.

The recent double burning of Ridley and Latimer helped to shape the burgeoning popular image of martyrdom. Both men died with the resolute piety that had come to be the hallmark of those the Catholic clergy called heretics. Ridley died slowly and horribly, his agony prolonged by a badly built fire. Latimer appeared to die all but painlessly, seeming miraculously to embrace the fire and bathe his hands and face in it. Many people in the large crowd that came to witness the executions wept and shook their heads at the sight, and carried away the memory of Latimer's prophecy that the meaning of these sufferings would become clear in time.

SOURCE: Carolly Erickson, historian and author of historical fiction and non-fiction, explaining reasons for Mary Tudor's reputation, from her biography, *Bloody Mary*, 1998

Summarize

What does it say about Mary and her reputation?

The document tells of popular songs that memorialized Protestant martyrs killed by Mary's officials. Erickson says that "ballad-makers" sang stories of 75 people burned as heretics, and their songs made heroes of the martyrs.

Analyze

Why does it matter to the question of Mary's reputation?

Although it is true that Mary's officials were responsible for the executions, it was the popularizing of these deaths by balladeers that helped to "enhance" the queen's reputation among her people. It is likely that many previous kings were responsible for an equal number of executions, but most were never burdened with the moniker *bloody*.

Criticize

Why does the source matter?

Since this document is from a late-twentieth-century biography of a sixteenth-century monarch, it is likely that Erickson had access to all the most recent research into Mary Tudor. All things being equal, you can expect the book to be a very measured account of Mary's reign. Of course, you probably would not know that Carolly Erickson has a reputation for being somewhat generous with her subjects, so she may have intended that readers would place some blame on the balladeers. That is not to say that the book is in any way unreliable as it likely went through a rigorous peer review process before publication, and you can read any number of reviews written after it was released.

Part 3: Textbooks and Encyclopedias

You already have had enough experience with history textbooks in your lifetime to know that they are generally no fun to read. Most often their style is intentionally dry and impersonal. Given the choice between reading a standard high school history textbook and watching paint dry, I'm taking the paint every time! But what if you don't have a choice? That is probably the situation in which you find yourself this year. Pre-AP and AP History courses almost certainly require some textbook reading. The good news is that, if you're in an AP or Pre-AP History class, you may already be pretty skilled with a textbook. Either way, if you encounter a document excerpted from a textbook or encyclopedia, you will definitely want to know how to apply your newfound skills for analyzing documents.

A great example of this type of writing is the *Encyclopedia Britannica*. With instant online access, the *Britannica* is a good place to begin your research. Let's say, for instance, that you were exploring the causes for the fall of Mussolini in twentieth-century Italy. Below is an excerpt from *Britannica*'s "Benito Mussolini" article. As you might expect from an encyclopedia article, it just highlights his career without going too deeply into the details. Read the document and use the 3-step process to analyze it in terms of the question, "In what ways did Benito Mussolini help to bring about his own demise?"

> Wounded while serving [in WWI] with the *bersaglieri* (a corps of sharpshooters), he returned home a convinced antisocialist and a man with a sense of destiny. As early as February 1918, he advocated the emergence of a dictator—"a man who is ruthless and energetic enough to make a clean sweep"—to confront the economic and political crisis then gripping Italy. Three months later,

in a widely reported speech in Bologna, he hinted that he himself might prove to be such a man. The following year the nucleus of a party prepared to support his ambitious idea was formed in Milan. In an office in Piazza San Sepolcro, about 200 assorted republicans, anarchists, syndicalists, discontented socialists, restless revolutionaries, and discharged soldiers met to discuss the establishment of a new force in Italian politics. Mussolini called this force the *fasci di combattimento* ("fighting bands"), groups of fighters bound together by ties as close as those that secured the fasces of the lictors—the symbols of ancient Roman authority. So fascism was created and its symbol devised.

At rallies—surrounded by supporters wearing black shirts—Mussolini caught the imagination of the crowds. His physique was impressive, and his style of oratory, staccato and repetitive, was superb. His attitudes were highly theatrical, his opinions were contradictory, his facts were often wrong, and his attacks were frequently malicious and misdirected; but his words were so dramatic, his metaphors so apt and striking, his vigorous, repetitive gestures so extraordinarily effective, that he rarely failed to impose his mood.

SOURCE: John Foot, Professor of Modern Italian History, University of Bristol, from "Benito Mussolini" in the *Encyclopedia Britannica*, 2018

Summarize

What does the document say about Benito Mussolini?

John Foot outlines the life experiences that led Mussolini to fascism. His disillusionment and disappointment with Italy's post-WWI situation led him to conclude that the country needed a strong leader and he thought he might just be the right person for the job. According to the document, Mussolini used ancient Roman symbols, theatrical speeches, misinformation, and vicious attacks on his opponents to win popular support.

Analyze

Analyze the document in terms of its relevance to the question of Mussolini's demise.

Although this document actually never gets into the fall of Mussolini, there are a few relevant pieces of evidence. In its description of the original members he banded together to form the *fasci di combattimento*, the document uses words like discontented and restless. If Mussolini rose to power with the backing of an angry mob thirsting for change, as this document suggests, then he might have been the victim of that same anger when he failed to deliver on some of his promises. Additionally, if those same discontented masses turned on him, they may have begun to recognize Mussolini's contradictions, misdirections, and outright lies. Using the evidence of the methods he used to gain power in Italy, you might find this document helpful in arguing that those very methods eventually brought him down.

Criticize

Is there anything in the source line that might impact your analysis?

Since the extent of our knowledge of John Foot is that he is a British professor of Modern Italian History, we really know very little about his personal agenda. It is likely, however, that the information in the article is based on years of professional study and that the arguments Foot makes are in the mainstream given the broad distribution of *Encyclopedia Britannica*.

Part 4: Charts and Graphs

The last document types we need to discuss are charts and graphs. *Math?!!!* Don't get nervous! Charts and graphs are essentially visual documents, so we will apply the 3-step process here in the same way we did in Unit 5. Describe what you see in the document and that description becomes your summary, then just Analyze and Criticize as you have with every other document in the book.

For our example, we will look at a graph of stock prices in Argentina and the U.S.A. between 1906 and 1930. In those years, Italians were leaving their homes in great numbers and emigrating to the Americas. Many of them landed in a newly-independent Argentina and made their livings as farmers, laborers, or professionals. The Argentine government did more than just welcome the immigrants, it legislated free land and tax breaks for any European who wanted to come. Was this a good idea for the Argentinians? Analyze the graph and consider the question, "To what extent was Italian immigration to Argentina a good deal for the Argentine economy?"

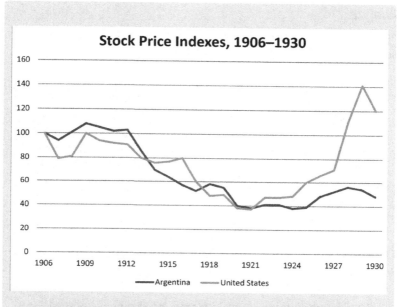

SOURCE: Leonard Nakamura, economic researcher,
Federal Reserve Bank of Philadelphia, from a working
paper analyzing early-twentieth-century stock prices in
Argentina, 1997

Summarize

Describe what you see in the graph?

The graph compares U.S. and Argentine stock prices
across 25 years (1906–1930). It shows that Argentine stock
prices compared favorably to those of U.S. stocks—even
outperforming them in the first 8 years—until about 1921
when U.S. stocks began to skyrocket.

Analyze

Analyze the document in terms of its relevance to the question about economic benefits for Argentina.

Since stock prices are often used as an indication of economic productivity, this document could be used to support the argument that the Argentine economy was healthy and productive during the years of the greatest immigration from Italy. Additionally, given what we know now about the U.S. stock market in the 1920s, even the last few years of the graph seem to support Argentine economic stability.

Criticize

Is there anything in the source line that might impact your analysis?

The graph is taken from a report by the U.S. Federal Reserve in 1997. By that date, it is likely that statisticians were working with reliable data from the first decades of the century.

You Try It: World History Textbook

Directions: For the exercise below, read the document and follow the instructions for each task. How might this document help us to better understand the success of the Vikings?

The Vikings' motives were announced in their name, which derives from the Old Norse *vik*, "to be on the warpath." The Vikings sought to loot the now wealthy Franks and replace them as the dominant warrior class of northern Europe. It was their turn to extract plunder and to sell droves of slaves across the water. They succeeded because of a deadly technological advantage: ships of unparalleled sophistication, developed by Scandinavian sailors in the Baltic Sea and the long fjords of Norway. Light and agile, with a shallow draft, they could penetrate far up the rivers of northern Europe and even be carried overland from one river system to another. Under sail, the same boats could tackle open water and cross the unexplored wastes of the North Atlantic.

In the ninth century, the Vikings set their ships on both courses. They emptied northern Europe of its treasure, sacking the great monasteries of Ireland and Britain and overlooking the Rhine and the Seine – rivers that led into the heart of Charlemagne's empire. At the same time, Norwegian adventurers colonized the uninhabited island of Iceland, and then Greenland. By 982 CE, they had reached the New World and established a settlement at L'Anse aux Meadows on the Labrador coast. Viking goods have been found as far west as the Inuit settlements of Baffin Island to the north of Hudson Bay, carried there along trading routes by Native Americans.

The consequences of this spectacular reach across the ocean to America were short-lived, but the penetration of eastern Europe had lasting effects. Supremely well-equipped to traverse long river systems, the Vikings sailed east along the Baltic and then turned south, edging up the rivers that crossed the watershed of central Russia. Here the Dnieper, the Don, and the Volga begin to flow south into the Black Sea and the Caspian. By opening this link between the Baltic and what is now Kiev in modern Ukraine, the Vikings created an avenue of commerce that linked Scandinavia and the Baltic directly to Constantinople and Baghdad. And they added yet more slaves: Muslim geographers bluntly called this route "The Highway of the Slaves."

SOURCE: Robert L. Tignor, Professor of Modern History, Princeton University, writing in collaboration with several other historians, *Worlds Together, Worlds Apart*, 2014

Summarize

What does the document say about the Vikings?

Analyze

Why might this document matter to a more thorough understanding of the reasons for Viking success?

Criticize

How might the date of this document help to assess our analysis of the text?

Answers and Explanations

Summarize

The document tells of the Vikings' use of ship technology to defeat their enemies and win control of new trade routes. The authors detail the innovations that allowed Viking sailors to move through the rivers of Europe as well as the open seas of the North Atlantic. This excerpt also details the sorts of goods the Vikings traded, including slaves.

Analyze

The technological details of Viking ships can be used to support the argument that their innovations gave them a distinct advantage over their landlubber competitors. You can imagine that in the 9th and 10th centuries, if you had ships that could be rowed upriver, sailed across the open sea, and carried across the land, you would definitely be the big dogs in town. The document's explanation for why the Vikings conducted their raids is also important to the reasons for their success. According to these authors, the Vikings were profit-seekers—they endeavored to control the trade routes formerly established under Charlemagne. This profit motive is easier to understand than the old bloodlust idea. Additionally, the Vikings used their advanced technology to create new trade routes connecting northern Europe with western Asia.

Criticize

Since this document comes from a textbook, you might be tempted to assume that it is "perfectly objective." If that's what you were thinking, I refer you back to Unit 1, Part 3—there are no objective documents. Every author has a perspective and every document is influenced by that perspective. Historians in particular are often attempting to tell a story, so they choose and present evidence in such a way as to support their version of history. In this case, although we know that Professor Tignor is a historian from Princeton University, because this textbook, like so many others, was written collaboratively with several unnamed historians, it would be difficult to comment on the authorship. Since it was published in 2014, it is likely based on the most current research, which may make it a more reliable source. Also, we could note the title, *Worlds Together, Worlds Apart*, which might suggest something about the story these authors have chosen to tell—one of convergence and divergence. Exchange networks might feature prominently in such a story, so that could prompt the writers to include more evidence about Vikings as traders.

Moving Forward

Well, that's it! You've finished *Mastering Document Analysis* and you're now ready to go apply the 3-Step Process on your own. As you continue to make your way through this world of information overload, don't get overwhelmed. Look at the evidence in front of you. What does it say? Why does it matter? Why might its source matter? Refer back to this book when you need help, but remember: *You Can Do This!* **Finding the past is as easy as 1-2-3—Summarize, Analyze, Criticize.**

Publisher's Acknowledgments

Over the 3+ years that this text was in development, we received feedback from many, many teachers—too many to name here. To all those who made a contribution, no matter how small, you have our sincere thanks. We would also like to thank Richard Carson for his editorial input in the early stages of this project.

Source Credits

Sherpa Learning, LLC has made every effort to obtain permission for the reprinting of all selections contained herein. If any owner of copyrighted material is not acknowledged herein, please contact the publisher for proper acknowledgement in all future editions or reprinting of this book.

(p. ix) Japanese flag photo credit: Tony Maccarella; (p. xiii) King, Ross. *Michelangelo and the Pope's Ceiling*. Random House, Oct 31, 2012; (p. 25) diary excerpt reprinted from *The Journal of Historical Review*, vol. 12, no. 1, pp. 31-85; (p. 28) National Archives; (p. 37) Blight, James G. & Janet M. Lang. *The Fog of War: Lessons from the Life of Robert S. McNamara*. Rowman & Littlefield Publishers, Mar 31, 2005; (p. 40) National Archives; (p. 42) Robespierre speech from *The Ninth of Thermidor: the Fall of Robespierre*, by Richard Bienvenu, Oxford University Press, Jan 1, 1968; (p. 54) from *The Guernsey Literary and Potato Peel Pie Society*, by Mary Ann Shaffer & Annie Barrows, Allen & Unwin, Jun 1, 2009; (p. 64) Scala/White Images/Art Resource, NY; (p. 67) Mahatma Gandhi, Mithuben Petit and Sarojini Naidu during the Salt Satyagraha of 1930, photographer unknown, image from commons. wikimedia.org; (p. 70) Thomas Nast, "The Big Thing," wood engraving, from *Harper's Weekly*, 20 April 1867, courtesy of The Mavis P. and Mary Wilson Kelsey Collection of Thomas Nast Graphics; (p. 73) Strothmann, loc. gov; (p. 79) Langworth, Richard M. *Churchill by Himself: The Life, Times and Opinions of Winston Churchill in His Own Words*. Ebury Publishing, Great Britain, 2008; (p. 80) from Crowley, Roger. *City of Fortune: How Venice Ruled the Seas*. New York: Random House, 2011. Kindle edition; (p. 82) Erickson, Carolly. *Bloody Mary*. New York: Macmillan, 1998; (p. 85) Foot, John, and Christopher Hibbert. "Benito Mussolini." *Encyclopædia Britannica*. Jul 25, 2018. Accessed Aug 20, 2018. https://www.britannica.com/biography/ Benito-Mussolini; (p. 89) Nakamura, Leonard I., and Carlos E.j.m. Zarazaga. "Banking and Finance in Argentina in the Period 1900-35." SSRN Electronic Journal, 2001. Accessed August 15, 2018. doi:10.2139/ssrn.274039; (p. 91) Tignor, Robert L., et al. *Worlds Together, Worlds Apart*. Fourth ed. New York: W.W. Norton & Company, 2014.

Author's Acknowledgments

Mastering Document Analysis grew out of a 45-minute workshop I presented in 2011. A particularly forward-thinking guy, David Nazarian, who was then a Project Manager for Peoples Education, thought my 3-Step Process would make a great new resource for history students. David, now my publisher, urged me to begin writing *MDA* for Sherpa Learning in 2013. He and I envisioned a new kind of educational resource—an ongoing collaboration with the teachers who use it. It was a grand concept and we set to work that winter—me writing the instructional material and David sharing it with anyone who would use it and give us feedback. Meanwhile, Sherpa and I published two versions of *Mastering the Essay*, and *MDA* took a back seat. Then in the spring of 2018, with David's encouragement, I dove back in to finish this amazing project.

So, I have to start by thanking David Nazarian for never giving up on me or this book! I'd also like to thank Christine DeFranco for pushing both of us to actually produce a finished product. Without David, I'm pretty sure this one would have shriveled on the vine, and without Christine, I'm pretty sure David and I would have talked about it for another seven years. Thanks to both of you for bringing *MDA* and *The Mastering Series* to life.

I know David will thank the dozens of teachers who used these exercises in draft form and provided the feedback we needed to make them even more useful for future teachers and students, but I would like to offer my own personal "Thank You!" And thanks to my friend and SRDS colleague, Kathy Philipp, for her last-minute wordsmithing advice.

My parents taught me the value of hard work and persistence, and Mom continues to live her life according to these standards. Thanks for being a great model, Mom. Although

Dad has been gone almost seven years now, I know he would be incredibly proud of this book. In addition to always setting the example for hard work, Dad liked to keep things simple. One of his favorite Dad-isms is a line he repeated whenever we built something. While I was busy pontificating about the specific character of every part of the project, Dad would always remind me, "Don't file it -- Nail it!" I'd like to believe that he would have appreciated the simplicity of Summarize, Analyze, Criticize.

Finally, I'd like to thank my wife, Christine, who continues to support a writing career that, while immensely fulfilling, doesn't exactly pay the bills. She helps me to carve out spare minutes in our hectic lives to continue these projects. Although my son, Ben, is off on his own family adventure with my daughter-in-law, Shannon, and my first granddaughter, Emma, his constant encouragement is as heartwarming as it is appreciated. My daughter, Mia, was in eighth grade when I started this book and will go off to college at the end of this year. Her amazing talent and positive spirit inspire me always to keep going, even in the face of the most persistent obstacles. She is the light of my life. Thanks to all of you!

Also by Tony Maccarella

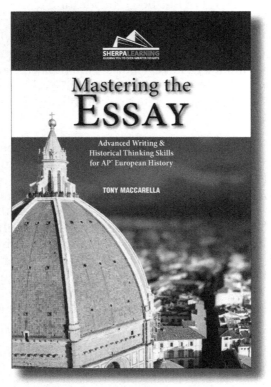

AP* European History Edition

Instructional Handbook: isbn 978-0-9905471-3-6
Exercise Workbook: isbn 978-0-9905471-4-3
Handbook/Workbook Combo: isbn 978-0-9905471-5-0

On the redesigned AP History exams, skills matter much more than memorized content. Written responses account for 60% of your final score. A new style of multiple-choice question requires you to quickly and correctly analyze historical documents. *Mastering the Essay* will equip you with ALL of the tools you need to move confidently through your AP History course and earn a 5 on the exam in May.

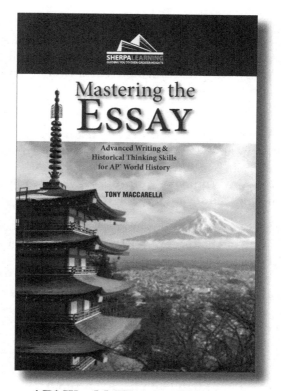

AP* World History Edition

Instructional Handbook: isbn 978-0-9905471-6-7
Exercise Workbook: isbn 978-0-9905471-8-1
Handbook/Workbook Combo: isbn 978-0-9905471-9-8

Mastering the Essay comes in two parts: an Instructional Handbook and an Exercise Workbook. The Workbook contains practice exercises designed to strengthen the skills introduced in the Instructional Handbook.

www.sherpalearning.com

About the Author

Tony Maccarella—or as students past and present call him, "Mr. Mac"—has been teaching social studies since 1982, and is currently teaching AP World History and AP Macroeconomics at Saddle River Day School, in Saddle River, NJ.

Prior to this, he taught AP European History at Parsippany Hills High School, in Parsippany, NJ for over 10 years. Additionally, Mr. Mac has taught AP U.S. History, Comparative Governments, Anthropology, Psychology, Microeconomics, and Military History.

Since 2002, Tony has served as a Reader and Table Leader for the AP European History exam for ETS. He is responsible for scoring AP European History exam questions, supervising other readers, and assisting with the clarification of scoring standards. You may also run into Tony at one of the many guest lecturer appearances he makes at social studies conferences across the Northeast.

Tony is an avid traveler. He has cycled across the United States, motorcycled to Sturgis and back, studied in China, and traveled throughout Italy with his wife, family, and students from seven different European History classes.

SHERPALEARNING

GUIDING YOU TO EVEN GREATER HEIGHTS

www.sherpalearning.com

Made in the USA
Columbia, SC
09 October 2020

22487779R00065